without whos[illegible] ould not
have been possible.

I am the land that listens,
I am the land that broods;
Steeped in eternal beauty,
crystalline waters and woods.
Long have I waited lonely,
shunned as a thing accursed,
Monstrous, moody, pathetic,
the last of the lands and the first;
Wild and wide are my borders,
stern as death is my sway,
And I wait for the men who will win me-
and I will not be won in a day.

The Law of the Yukon, Robert Service.

Rocky
Mountain Books

NOT WON IN A DAY

Climbing Canada's Highpoints

Jack Bennett

Front cover: Greg Borges at the top of the headwall on Mount Logan with King Peak in the background.
Back cover: The author at the top of Mount McKinley.
Double title page: Looking across the ice cap from the col south of Mount Barbeau. Photo Tony Daffern.

Lines from poems by Robert Service pages 9, 17 from *The Call of the Wild*, pages 14, 33, 53 from *The Law of the Yukon*, page 40 from *The Three Voices*, page 48 from *Men of the High North*, page 65 from *The Spell of the Yukon*, page 75 from *The Three Voices* and page 86 from *To the Man of the High North*.

The author acknowledges route descriptions supplied by others:
Mount Logan, East Ridge (p.107), Brian Cabe, Salt Lake City, UT;
Mount Fairweather, Carpé Ridge (p.115), John Imbrie, Keswick, VA;
White Hill, Lake of Islands (p.147), Greg Slayden, Seattle, WA.

Mountain sketches Tan Rambo.

We acknowledge the financial support of the Government of Canada through the Book Publishing Industry Development Program (BPIDP) for our publishing activities.
Canada

Printed and bound in Canada by
Houghton Boston, Saskatoon

RMB
Published by
Rocky Mountain Books
#4 Spruce Centre SW
Calgary, Alberta T3C 3B3

ISBN 0-921102-70-4

Canadian Cataloguing in Publication Data

Bennett, Jack, 1943-
Not won in a day

Includes index.
ISBN 0-921102-70-4

1. Mountaineering--Canada. I. Title.
GV199.44.C2B46 1999 76.5'22'0971 C99-911020-9

Contents

The Story

The Guide

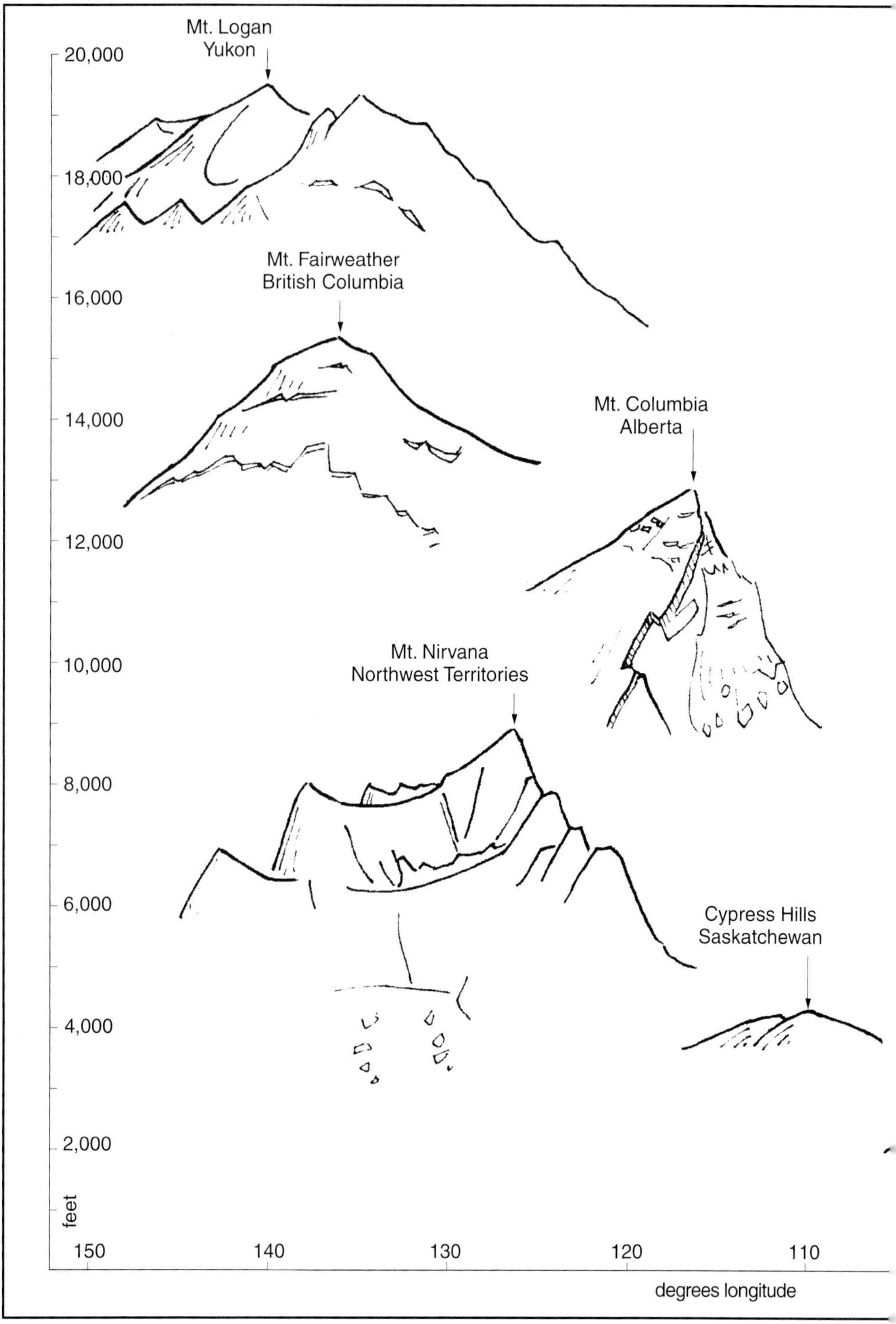

Mt. Logan
Yukon
Mt. Fairweather
British Columbia
Mt. Columbia
Alberta
Mt. Nirvana
Northwest Territories
Cypress Hills
Saskatchewan
20,000
18,000
16,000
14,000
12,000
10,000
8,000
6,000
4,000
2,000
feet
150
140
130
120
110
degrees longitude

The Highpoints of Canada

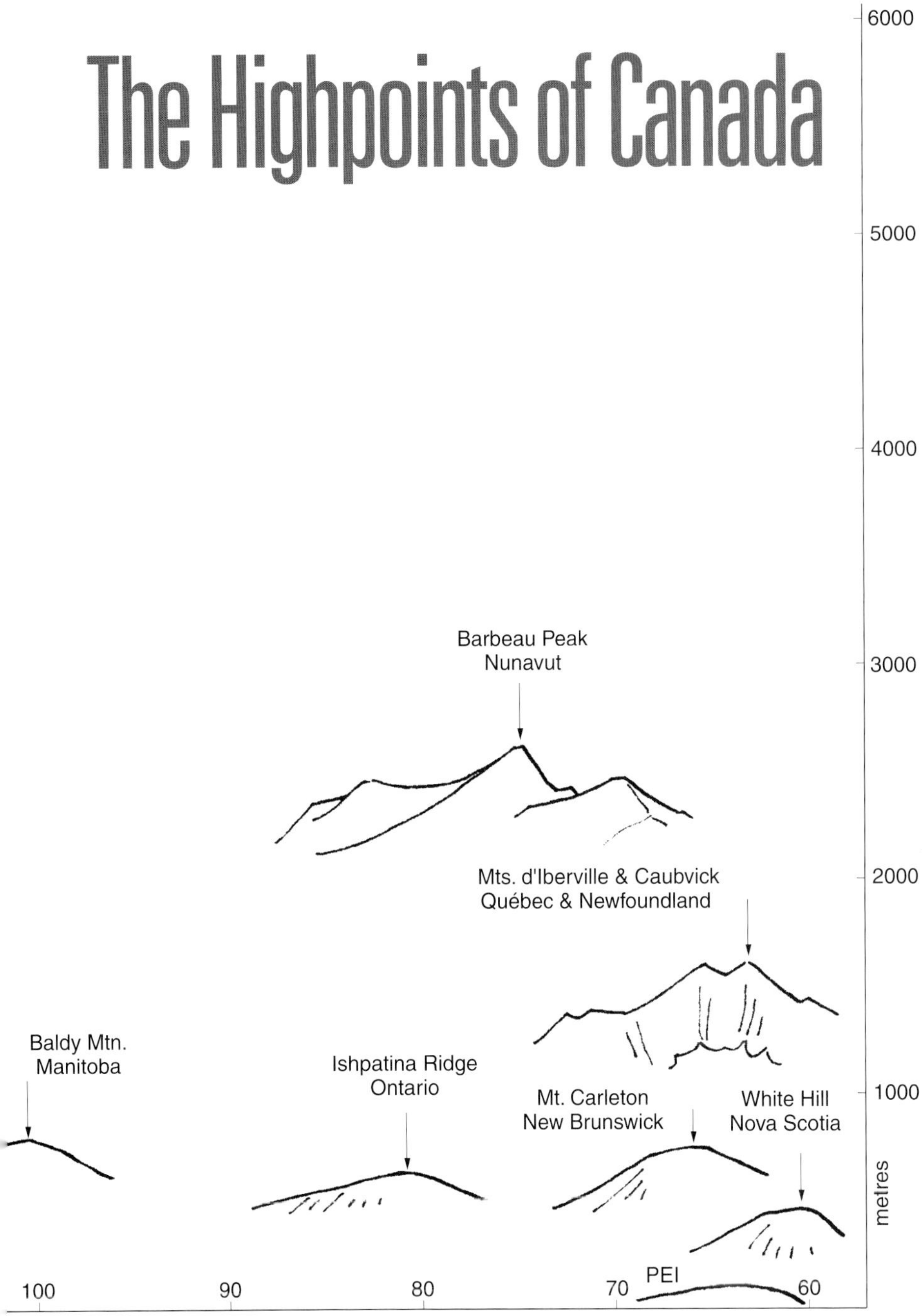

Arctic Ocean
Barbeau Peak
Barrow
Nome
Beaufort Sea
Fort Yukon
Tuktoyaktuk
Fairbanks
Anchorage
Valdez
Cordova
YUKON
Mt. Logan
Whitehorse
Mt. Fairweather
Mt. Nirvana
Juneau
Port Radium
NUNAVUT
Yellowknife
NORTHWEST TERRITORIES
Baker Lake
Rankin Inlet
Gulf of Alaska
BRITISH COLUMBIA
Prince Rupert
Dawson Creek
ALBERTA
Fort Chipewyan
Fort McMurray
Grande Prairie
Prince George
SASKATCHEWAN
Edmonton
Mt. Columbia
North Battleford
Prince Albert
Kamloops
Vancouver
Victoria
Kelowna
Calgary
Saskatoon
Trail
Lethbridge
Swift Current
Cypress Hills
Brandon
Flin Flon
MANITOBA
Baldy Mtn.
Winnipeg
Churchill
Hudson Bay
Baffin Bay
BAFFIN ISLAND
Siglufjordhur
Reykjavik
Ikateq
North Atlantic Ocean
Nanortalik
Labrador Sea
Mt. d'Iberville
Mt. Caubvick
Inukjuak
Labrador City
Corner Brook
St. John's
QUEBEC
ONTARIO
Moosonee
Thunder Bay
Timmins
Ishpatina Ridge
Sudbury
Amos
North Bay
Ottawa
Kingston
Toronto
Trois-rivieres
Montreal
Quebec
Mt. Carleton
Charlottetown
PEI
White Hill
Sydney
Fredericton
Halifax
Bangor

Finished!

Let us probe the silent places,
let us seek what luck betides us;
Let us journey to a lonely land I know.
There's a whisper on the night-wind,
there's a star agleam to guide us,
And the wild is calling, calling…let us go.

Stuart was only a rope length away, standing on the summit. I could hardly believe I was almost there. My head pounded with every beat of my heart and my legs had turned to jelly. I was suffering from acute mountain sickness, and every step seemed an effort beyond belief.

Stuart Ferguson, my son Tom and I had decided to attempt the summit of Mount McKinley from our little campsite at 4880 metres (16,000 ft.), an ambitious and perhaps foolish decision. Most climbers summit from a camp at the Crow's Nest at 5240 metres (17,200 ft.), and very few attempt anything more. Our plans called for an all-out assault, gaining 1300 metres (4300 ft.) to reach the summit at 6190 metres (20,300 ft.). It had been a mean spring on McKinley. Only two people had reached the summit in the last two weeks, and all who tried reported howling 128 kilometre (80 mi.) per hour winds and deep drifting snow. Then came the miracle, a perfect day with clear skies and calm winds. Such a day would not come again soon. Stuart, Tom and I set out in the bitter morning cold.

At Denali Pass, 5640 metres (18,500 ft.), Tom nearly passed out from the pain of an intense altitude headache, a possible sign of cerebral edema. Tom's summit day was over, and after shedding a few tears he sadly started back to camp. How my heart ached for him! But my ordeal was just beginning. The climb to the summit of Mount McKinley was the hardest and most painful I had ever known, and my condition deteriorated with every step. Stuart was patient with me and did what he could to help, but each step seemed equal to my worst nightmare. Finally I struggled to the top of North

The author struggling to the summit of Mount McKinley in 1990. With this ascent he became the twelfth person to climb all 50 US highpoints.

America: Mount McKinley, Denali, The Great One. Stuart and I embraced and I wept like a baby. It was 8:00 pm on June 4, 1990. I had just reached the highpoint of my 50th state, a project that had taken me 18 years to complete. So many memories drifted through my mind; so many memories....

When I was 12 years old my father took me to the summit of Mount Davis, the highest point in Pennsylvania. A fire tower reached just above the surrounding trees. It was not exactly a breathtaking view. The mountaintop was flat, and many vistas along the Appalachian Mountain chain were more impressive. Even so, I remember being fascinated. This place was unique, and for a brief moment I too was unique. Nowhere in the whole state of Pennsylvania was there anyone higher than I. It was not a feeling of power or achievement, but the idea that together with this place, I was somehow special. This was not insignificant to a skinny, funny-looking kid who felt special in no other way. It made a lasting impression on me.

Later, at the age of 30, I stood on the summit of Mount Mitchell with my wife Nancy and two young sons, Dan and Tom. Mount Mitchell, at 2038 metres (6684 ft.), is the highest point in North Carolina and the highest point east of the Mississippi River. At that moment I decided to stand atop as many state highpoints as possible. Each year we vacationed in a different part of the country, and slowly our highpoint total mounted. Many of the highpoints were nothing more than silly. The highpoint of Indiana was in a field of soybeans. The highpoint of Iowa was in a feed lot, just behind a farmer's barn. And I certainly wouldn't recommend the highpoints of Delaware, Louisiana or Kansas for majestic views!

But along with the ridiculous came the sublime. We learned the techniques of rock climbing and belaying for Gannet Peak, Wyoming, and Granite Peak, Montana. And we learned ice climbing and crevasse rescue for Mount Hood, Oregon, and Mount Rainier, Washington. We bivouacked through a bitterly cold night with little protection on Froze-to-Death Mountain in Montana, and we were lucky to escape without injury from a deadly storm high on the Exum Ridge of the Grand Teton. It took us three tries to bag the summit of Gannet Peak in Wyoming.

It had all led like a river to this moment at the summit of Mount McKinley. I was the 12th person to climb the highest points of all 50 states. I was reminded of what Roald Amundson said to his fellow Norwegians upon being the first person to reach the South Pole. "I must confess, I have no profound thoughts to share with you at this moment," he said. "Only, how good it is to be alive!"[1]

How good it was to be alive indeed! To the northeast, the tongue of the Muldro Glacier probed far out into the Alaskan tundra in an endless search for the sea. Directly to the north, the black rocks of the north summit of Denali, only a little over 250 metres (800 ft.) lower than where we stood, concealed an abrupt drop of 4000 metres (13,000 ft.) to the Peters Glacier below. Mount Foraker, itself the fifth highest mountain in North America, floated above a sea of clouds to the southwest. And to the south, the ridges and walls of the incredible south face of Mount McKinley rose directly to the summit where we stood. Here were the great routes that climbers dream of; the Cassin Ridge and the south face of Denali. Compared to those celebrated climbs, our route had been a walk in the park, but at this moment it was enough. A great contentment swept over me. How I would have loved to share this moment with Tom.

Whenever I had reached a summit in the past, the effort was over. After a little rest we would hurry down, laughing and sliding all the way. But something was clearly different this time. I was sick, and even going downhill every step seemed more than I could manage. I began to hallucinate, watching spiders scurry across the snow in front of me. Sometimes I would pause to brush them from my shoulders. These apparitions both intrigued and appalled me. I knew that they were only illusions, but their seeming realism was fascinating to me. I also had the impression that bad things were happening in my brain, and that countless brain cells were dying by the minute! It took all the concentration I could muster to carefully place each foot on the ice without tripping and falling. I reminded myself constantly that most accidents happen during the descent, when minds are slow and bodies are spent. Not until we were almost back to camp did I begin to recover. And then came one of those magic moments of the mountains. It was 1:00 am, and we were descending the airy arête of the West Buttress. Clouds swirled up from the Peters Glacier below to be illuminated by the full moon and the glow of the arctic night. The effect was surreal and lovely! Anyone who has been in such a place at such a time would never ask why people climb mountains.

When we finally reached our tent 21 hours after leaving it, Tom was in a deep funk. Not only had he failed to reach the summit of McKinley, but he hadn't been able get the stove running and had had nothing to eat or drink all day. It was a bitter pill for Tom. All the way up the mountain he had hauled loads like a mule. On two occasions he had carried his load to camp, then come back down to carry my pack the last few hundred metres. Who would have guessed that I would reach the summit and he would fail? We talked briefly about trying again tomorrow, but Stuart and I both knew that neither one of us had the strength to go up again. Then, after a brief 24-hour window of good weather, McKinley slammed the door shut. Sometime before dawn the tent began to tremble, and we were soon in the teeth of a serious blizzard. We decided to descend quickly to the relative safety of the ice bowl at 4390 metres (14,400 ft.). It seemed a safe decision. After all, the warden had told us that no one had ever died in an avalanche on the West Buttress route. As it turned out, we were almost the first.

We could hardly see each other through the blizzard as we descended a fixed rope on the steep headwall of the West Buttress. The Park Service had fastened two lines of rope on the headwall, and to our left two other figures were descending through the storm. These were two German climbers, whom we knew only as Hans and George. They had ascended more or less alongside us, camped next to us at 4880 metres (16,000 ft.), and summited on the same day as Stuart and I. Now we were all desperately hurrying down the ropes to safety.

Suddenly, Tom, who was at the top of our rope, yelled "Avalanche. Hold on!" I had failed to clip my climbing harness onto the fixed rope, so I hastily wrapped my arm around the rope and held on for life. The avalanche swept over us. When the snow stopped flowing, we were still on the rope, but badly shaken. Not as shaken as Hans and George, however. "Zis is dangerous! Ve go up. Ve go up!" Hans shouted. "We go down!" I replied, and we doubled our speed down the ropes toward the ice bowl. Hans and George hesitated only a moment, then began descending too.

After a few minutes Tom yelled "Another avalanche. Hold on!" This one was bigger, and I fought to keep my grip as the flowing snow tried to tear us from the rope. Finally it was over, but when I looked to my left Hans and George were gone. The avalanche had pulled them from the rope, but as Hans had clipped his climbing harness around the rope, they came to a jolting stop at the next anchor point. Hans was buried, but was able to uncover himself. George was on his back with his head downhill, but still above the snow. George screamed, "Stuart, help me!" I was amazed, as these were the only English words I had ever heard George utter. Some equipment was lost, and Hans was slightly injured, but we were all alive and quickly resumed our descent. The outcome could have been much worse.

After waiting out the storm in the ice bowl, we began the long trek down the Kahiltna Glacier and back to the comforts of civilization.

I was thrilled to have bagged my 50th highpoint, but after a few days of euphoria, the thrill began to wear off. My hobby of the past 18 years was over. I was finished. No more planning next year's trip. No more poring over maps and pictures to rehearse every detail of the climb. I was finished! I began to feel depressed. I needed a new challenge in my life.

In 1983 a wealthy Texas oilman named Dick Bass conceived of the "Seven Summits," a plan to climb to the highest point of each of the seven continents in a single year. The very idea was preposterous! Dick Bass was over 50 years old. No one that old had ever climbed Mount Everest, the highest point of Asia. And to make it even more absurd, Dick Bass was not an experienced mountain climber. Many felt that he had not paid his dues to climb the world's tallest peaks. But three years later, Dick Bass had indeed become the first person to step on the highest point of all seven continents. His book, *The Seven Summits*, became popular reading, not so much because of the physical feat of what he had done, but because it bridged the seemingly enormous gap between the elite mountain climbers of the world and ordinary mortals. Dick Bass, by showing us what can be accomplished by sheer will, was an inspiration to thousands. Today many people, both men and women, have followed in his footsteps and completed the seven summits. Many others are still trying.

Did I have the determination and physical ability to climb the seven summits? Maybe, but unfortunately it takes more than determination and hard work to climb to the highest points of all seven continents. It takes very deep pockets! The going rate for a climb of Mount Everest was $65,000. If it took three tries to succeed, as it did Dick Bass, multiply that by three! The Vinson Massif in Antarctica is nearly as expensive. To climb the seven summits today, a person would need at least a quarter of a million dollars. Not many people have that kind of liquid assets. I certainly didn't.

I also found the idea of hiring a guide to lead me up a mountain distasteful. Most of the people attempting the seven summits hire the best mountain guides in the world. Going guided completely changes the dynamics of the group. The guide makes all the decisions for the party—when to go on and when to turn back, when and where to camp, when and what to eat, etc. Guides have even been known to "short-rope" clients, attaching a rope to them and hauling them up. The client depends on the guide to get him to the top, and, if necessary, to rescue him. This system is extremely risky, especially on Everest, and lately both clients and guides have been dying at an alarming rate.

Don't get me wrong. I have the utmost respect for anyone who can keep putting one foot in front of the other above 8000 metres (26,200 ft.) to reach the summit of Mount Everest. But it was not a scene I wanted to be a part of, even if I had had the money. My sons, Dan and Tom, and I had always made our own decisions and had done our own work on the mountains we climbed. Sometimes we made bad decisions, and sometimes we paid the price. But right or wrong, the decisions and the summits were ours. No one else took the blame when we failed, and no one else claimed credit when we succeeded.

I needed a goal closer to home, one affordable for the everyday climber or adventurer and yet challenging enough to test our skill and resolve. And so it was that I began to wonder about the highpoints of Canada: the highest points of all 12 Canadian provinces and territories. That, I reasoned, we could do ourselves, and without spending an arm and a leg.

When I was a child, each year our family made an annual fishing pilgrimage to Ontario. In those days, before the construction of the interstate highways, it was a long and tedious journey from Pennsylvania to Canada. My father carefully serviced and packed the car, attending to every last detail. My sister, Joan, and I snuggled into the bed my father constructed for us in the back seat. Often we left before dawn to avoid the traffic jams in Buffalo and Toronto.

To my young eyes, Canada was a magical land of crystalline waters and untracked wilderness. Every year I looked forward with grand anticipation to that day when we would cross the Peace bridge and make our way north to little Lake Cecebe on the Magnetawan River. Here we would spend the week fishing and swimming to our heart's content. The rustic cabin where we stayed had an unforgettable smell of pine and smoke. There was no electricity—a step back in time that didn't exactly thrill my mother. We cooked on a wood stove, read by kerosene lamp, and hid our fish treasures in secret caches in an icehouse filled with sawdust and blocks of winter ice. For me, Canada was a land of wonder and enchantment, and so it remains today. The Canadian highpoints seemed a natural and beautiful extension of the US highpoints, but for me they were also a return to that excitement and anticipation I felt in my youth.

A little research soon told me that the Canadian highpoints would be a bigger challenge than I had first imagined. No one had ever succeeded in climbing all of the Canadian highpoints, and for good reason. At least four of the summits are difficult world-class mountain climbs. The most difficult Canadian highpoint is actually harder from a technical viewpoint than any of the seven summits. Others are in wild and remote places. Only three of the Canadian highpoints are relatively easy to approach by road. The rest are untamed, mysterious places of snow, ice and polar bears! I am an admirer of Robert W. Service, and an excerpt from his poem aptly describes my impression of many of the Canadian highpoints:

I am the land that listens,
I am the land that broods;
Steeped in eternal beauty,
crystalline waters and woods.
Long have I waited lonely,
shunned as a thing accursed,
Monstrous, moody, pathetic,
the last of the lands and the first;
Wild and wide are my borders,
stern as death is my sway,
And I wait for the men who will win me—
and I will not be won in a day.

And so it was, with an almost forgotten sense of awe and excitement, that I began planning to climb the Canadian highpoints. My son Tom immediately signed on for the entire project. Dan, who was concentrating on a college degree, could not join an expedition every year, but would come when he could.

Nancy and I first began dragging Dan and Tom to highpoints when they were only four and two years old. They have little memory of those early highpoints, which were mostly the easy, drive-up highpoints of the eastern United States. But both accomplished remarkable climbs as they grew older. Each year I would stuff the old Dodge wagon full of gear, and we would head off to another part of the country. Tom was a reluctant climber as a child, always complaining and dragging behind, and taking every opportunity to flop down and rest. He needed constant reassurance, and doubted his ability to achieve anything. But once we reached a summit, he would disappear downhill at breakneck speed, not to be seen again until we reached the car. As Tom got older he matured into a determined and competent climber, far more skilled and capable than I. He embraced the outdoor life, becoming a white-water guide and climbing instructor for outdoor adventure companies. I watched with pride as Tom's skills grew, and he matured both physically and spiritually into a confident, self-assured young man.

Dan was different from the start. He always seemed to have self confidence and a sense of purpose. Even as a child, he wasted little time worrying about what others might think of him. He never cared much for material comforts, but seemed to possess an inner peace that I envied. Dan was easygoing and friendly, but also had a dogged determination to reach his goal, whatever it might be. In 1995 he was diagnosed with Crohn's disease, an insidious affliction of the small intestine that strikes young people and those over 50. So far, there is no cure for this disease. But even after emergency surgery, during which 15 centimetres (6 in.) of Dan's small intestine were removed, his attitude remained positive and unshaken.

Today, Dan and Tom have both reached the highest points of 49 US states, lacking only Mount McKinley, Alaska. Sharing these experiences with my two sons has been one of the greatest joys of my life. We have planned together, worked together, failed and succeeded, laughed and wept together. We have experienced more joy and sorrow on these climbs than I thought could ever be held in one lifetime.

A highpointer is a unique type of individual. He is a list-keeper, consumed with detail, and very goal oriented. To a highpointer, the summit is the tangible, undeniable measure of success in a world where success is all too often subjective and ill defined. There is nothing quite so satisfying as pursuing and attaining a difficult goal. The goal is what keeps a highpointer going through deprivation and often unbelievable hardship. An often-quoted excerpt from the poem *If*, by Kipling, deserves mention here:

If you can force your heart, and nerve, and sinew
To serve your turn long after they are gone,
And so hold on, when there is nothing in you
Except the will that says to them, "Hold on!"

Some of the Canadian highpoints need that kind of spirit. Make no mistake! If you challenge the Canadian highpoints they will sometimes require all that is in you. They will not be won in a day. But the satisfaction of reaching your goal will be as great as the dedication you put into it.

I climb for the risk as well as the goal. How well I remember when, as a child, I was enthralled by the story of Thor Hyerdahl crossing the Pacific Ocean on the tiny balsa raft Kon Tiki. Later I immersed myself in the stories of the great polar explorers Friedoff Nansen, Roald Amundsen, Scott and Shackelton. How I longed to be a part of their journeys! Our lives today so easily become rote, filled only with jobs, television and housework. How I treasure those few days each year when I savour the adventure and risk of the mountains.

Yet the mountains are for me much more than a challenge. They are mystical places of profound beauty and spiritual growth. It is surely no accident that religions all over the world associate high places with God and a renewal of the spirit. For me, all the elements of a major climb—beauty, challenge, hardship, isolation, even suffering—combine to create a spiritual experience that I can find in no other way. Life has acquired more meaning for me because of those few occasions when I have travelled to the very edge, and gazed into the mysterious unknown beyond.

When we began climbing highpoints in 1973, I had no idea that anyone else would be interested in such an endeavour. But highpointing has today become a popular North American pastime. The Highpointers Club has over 1900 members, and at last count 74 people have visited the summits of all 50 states. The Highpointers Club was founded and is still directed by its tireless president, Jack Longacre. The address of the club is:

The Highpointers Club
c/o Jack Longacre,
Box 327
Mountain Home, AR
72653 USA
www.highpointers.com

[1] "The Last Place on Earth," (videocassettes), BFS Video, Richmond Hill, Ontario, 1994.

Mount Logan, The Icy Giant

One by one I dismayed them,
frighting them sore with my glooms;
One by one I betrayed them
into my manifold dooms.
Burst with my winter upon them,
searing forever their sight,
Lashed them with fungus-white faces,
whimpering wild in the night....

Tom and I silently watched the Cessna disappear like a little red mosquito into the vast wilderness of the Icefield Ranges. We had just finished our flight from Kluane Lake over rank upon rank of barren icy mountains of the Saint Elias Range, and finally past the incredible Hummingbird Ridge of Mount Logan itself. When the whining sound of the plane's engine had finally faded, we turned and looked at each other. Though no words were spoken, we communicated volumes. "Good Lord! What have we gotten ourselves into now?" We were utterly alone on the Quintino-Sella Glacier, 2740 metres (9000 ft.) above sea level on the flanks of Mount Logan, the most massive mountain in the world. We felt more isolated and defenseless than we had ever felt before, certainly more so than on Denali, where huge tent cities inhabit the mountain and hoards of climbers beat a virtual alpine freeway up the West Buttress. We felt intimidated and apprehensive. Every climber knows the story of the first ascent of Mount Logan, led by Allen Carpé in 1925. It is perhaps the most extraordinary epic of hardship and suffering in the annals of North American mountaineering, and we were attempting the very same route. What would the next few days hold for us? What hardship, exhilaration, tragedy or joy, what failure or success?

The Canadian highpoints were still like a dream to me, and I hadn't yet fully committed to the project. I felt that Mount Logan was the key. "If I can only succeed here," I told myself, "then I'll have a shot. Then I'll go for all

12." But now, seeing the colossal size of this icy giant, and feeling so small standing in its shadow, I had serious doubts about my ability to scale it.

My life had been thrown into turmoil in 1987. My marriage of 22 years had failed, and suddenly not all things were possible. Nancy had herself climbed 48 US highpoints with me, often resigning herself to my whims, but it was not enough glue to hold a failing relationship together. It was the greatest sorrow of my life.

But out of failure also came a new beginning. A new friend, Mary Fran, was the most caring person I had ever met. She was the manager of a local library, and was engaged in the most awe-inspiring journey I could imagine. She was attempting to adopt a child as a single parent, a mission that would take her three years of seemingly endless paperwork and red tape. The options for single parent adoption were limited, and Mary Fran was working with agencies in India, Guatemala and Honduras. Finally, a call came in the middle of the night that a baby from an orphanage in India would be arriving for her on a Northwest flight from Minneapolis. I witnessed the joyous delivery at Cleveland Hopkins Airport on May 31, 1989. The baby, packed in a little wicker basket for her journey, looked to me like a beautiful little princess, and my heart was won forever. I married Mary Fran on September 1, 1990, and later also adopted Jennifer Rachana Bennett as my daughter, nearly 20 years after Tom was born.

Mary Fran was by no means an outdoors person, but she understood my love for the mountains and supported my occasional need to return to them despite the risk. She knew that the dangers on Mount Logan were more significant because of the isolation and difficulty of rescue. And now, standing at the foot of this icy giant, I felt an even greater responsibility to return home safely to Mary Fran and Jenny.

Soon the Cessna, piloted by Andy Williams of Icefield Ranges Expeditions, appeared again and deposited two more climbers on the glacier. The little red plane went back and forth all day until the seven climbers were together. Usually a climb of this scale requires a close-knit group of experienced mountaineers. Instead, we were a hodgepodge group that assembled that day on the Quintino-Sella Glacier. We had varying degrees of experience and background, and several of us had not even met until we gathered at the little airport in Whitehorse on May 31, 1992. Now, after a frustrating two-day delay owing to bad flying weather, we were poised at the foot of perhaps the greatest challenge of our lives.

Jerry and Jeff Wagener, another father-son highpointer team from Tulsa, Oklahoma, were the first to join Tom and me on the glacier. Both had already climbed all 50 US highpoints, and were, in fact, the first father-son duo to accomplish the feat. Jeff was a strong climber. Tall, lean and muscular, he had a mop of curly hair and an infectious smile. There was little doubt of his strength and confidence. His father was another matter, however. Jerry was quiet and unassuming, an instantly likable kindred spirit. But he was 54 years old, and it remained to be seen how he would withstand the rigours of such a climb.

Greg Borges, Warren Grill and Dave Peterson rounded out our original roster. Greg, Warren and Dave were in their twenties, and had all trained hard for the climb. These three had been friends as post-graduate students at Case-Western Reserve Medical School, though Dave had recently moved on to Minneapolis. I instantly liked Dave. He was friendly and quiet, but strong and intensely determined. The strength of his legs had earned him the nickname "Thunderthighs," a title bestowed on him by Warren and Greg. Dave, Warren and Greg, whom we called "The Three Musketeers," all seemed confident and strong for the climb ahead.

The final two members of our expedition, two Canadians we knew only by name as Ihor Zalubniak and Mauro Conzati, were already somewhere on the mountain. Ihor and Mauro were allowed to join our party when their own expedition fell apart, leaving them short of the required minimum of four climbers. Somehow they managed to talk Andy Williams into flying them in before we arrived, and then headed straight up the mountain without us! This was clearly against Parks Canada rules, not to mention bad judgment. It might not have been so distressing, except that they took the radio, our only link to the outside world. For Ihor and Mauro, we seemed to be only a convenient access onto the mountain, and they continued to act independently for the next three weeks. But Ihor was supremely confident and a very strong climber. His strength would prove to be invaluable to us later on.

Our expedition of nine was divided into four small cliques. Each clique ate together, tented together, roped together and climbed together. There was almost nothing that we all did as a group. Looking back, I can see that was a serious mistake. It bred disagreement and suspicion, and introduced me to divisive group dynamics, which I had never before experienced. The problems were obvious even before we flew in, when the team got together to discuss strategy on the mountain. "If someone gets hurt or sick," everyone reasoned, "then it's up to his tent mate to help him down." No one was willing to risk his shot at the summit to help someone else. I must admit that I was so focused on reaching the top that I bought in to this "every man for himself" attitude.

From our little camp on the glacier, a thin line of bamboo wands disappeared into the distance toward the King Trench. We were not alone on Mount Logan that year. A strong group of climbers led by Patrick Morrow was on the mountain ahead of us, with the objective of using GPS to determine the exact altitude of Mount Logan's summit. By now we were all anxious to get started, so Greg led off, following the trail of wands toward the trench. Greg, Warren and Dave were roped together, followed by a rope of Jerry, Jeff, Tom and me. Greg set a good pace, and we all followed, eager to prove ourselves against the mountain and to each other.

Here the glacier was not steep, so we used the time-honoured method of hauling loads that was first developed on Mount McKinley. As each climber starts out with about 54 kilograms (120 lbs.) of food, fuel and supplies, each advance up the mountain requires two carries. A load is first carried up to a

Hauling loads up the King Trench.

Climbers at the top of the headwall.

cache, then the climbers return to camp for the night. Camp is moved up the next day. This technique of "carry high, sleep low" assists in acclimatization. Flat-bottomed plastic sleds are usually used to take the excessive load off the climber's back, and make hauling much easier. These sleds are usually attached to the back of the climber's pack with a carabiner and nylon webbing. This is not as simple as it may seem. First, the sled has the temperament of a mule, and will invariably tip over if towed across a hill. Of course, the sled must be prevented from running over the climbing rope, and this is done by passing the rope under bungee cords on top of the sled. Also, should the climber plunge into a crevasse, the sled must be prevented from crashing down onto the head of the hapless climber. This is supposedly accomplished by attaching the back of the sled to the climbing rope with a prussik or butterfly knot, so that the climber behind can arrest it. It is mind-bogglingly complicated! The theory is that if a climber breaks through into a crevasse and finds himself hanging upside down in space with a 27-kilogram (60 lbs.) pack on his back and 14-18 additional kilograms (30-40 lbs.) dangling from his back, he simply takes off his pack and sled and clips them to the rope. He then ascends the rope using prussik knots or mechanical ascenders. If the climber is injured or unconscious, the crew on top must pull him up using a Z-pulley with multiple anchors set up on the glacier. Give me a break! If I ever fall into a crevasse with all that misfortune I only hope that I die quickly.

As we ascended the glacier the grade increased, and the trail skirted huge yawning crevasses. Jerry soon began puffing and wheezing like an old steam engine, often asking for a rest. Still, Greg pushed the pace until we reached a small cramped campsite at about 3050 metres (10,000 ft.) where we could cache our loads. The first 3.5 kilometre (2 mi.) carry was fast, two hours up and only one hour down. Back at base camp on the Quintino-Sella Glacier, everyone wondered if Jerry was up to the task, and Jerry was silently angry with himself for being so slow.

The next morning dawned bright and clear, and we quickly moved camp up to the little site at 3050 metres (10,000 ft.). From here we made another 3.5 kilometre (2 mi.) carry up to King Trench camp on a broad plateau at 3380 metres (11,100 ft.), then returned for the night at 3050 metres (10,000 ft.). Everyone was now getting used to the treadmill: first one foot, then the other, then the next, synchronized to the rhythm of our own breathing. The rise of the glacier was gradual here, and Jerry seemed to be adapting to the drudgery. It was becoming clear that success on Mount Logan would not come from climbing skill or talent, but from sheer dogged determination.

The next day, June 5, we moved up to King Trench camp. Pat Morrow's expedition had built a palace here. Several tent sites had been dug into the glacier, and some ambitious architect had constructed an igloo roomy enough for several people. King Trench camp held another pleasant surprise for us: our radio! We discovered later that Ihor and Mauro, the wayward duo of our expedition, hadn't been able to make the radio work, and had left it behind in disgust. Above King Trench camp rose a steep icefall gaining over

300 metres (1000 ft.) of elevation. Fortunately, there was a smooth crevasse-free ramp leading up the centre, but still, it looked like a hump.

The next day dawned cloudless with a brilliant sun, and we carried a load to a cache at 3800 metres (12,500 ft.). The ramp wore on me as we switchbacked up in the burning sun. It was the first day that I felt drained by the continuous exertion and sunglare. The park warden in Haines Junction had advised us not to camp in this area because of the danger of avalanches, which thunder almost continuously down the north face of King Peak, so we stashed our loads and hurried back down the ramp. Just before heading down, I thought I caught a glimpse of two small figures moving toward the pass high above us. Could this be the elusive Ihor/Mauro duo? I was beginning to wonder if they were real, or a kind of Mount Logan "Kilroy was here." The more adventurous decided to ride their sleds down the ramp to King Trench camp, while the more cautious of us plodded into camp long after the sledders had arrived.

June 7 was the most demanding day yet, as we moved camp all the way from King Trench camp to King Col at 4100 metres (13,500 ft.), a gain of 730 metres (2400 ft.) in elevation over a distance of five kilometres (3 mi.). Again we pushed up the ramp and on to our cache from the day before. After a brief rest, we headed toward King Col. It was snowing heavily on the mountain, and Tom led all the way to the col, breaking trail through deep snow. At the col were none other than Ihor Zalubniak and Mauro Conzati, the long-lost members of our expedition! Ihor excitedly began directing manoeuvres like a traffic cop. "A small tent can go right here. Put the big tent over there!" He exuded enthusiasm and confidence from every pore. Ihor's positive attitude was infectious, and I liked him despite his apparent indifference to park rules.

We awoke the next day to find a 25-centimetre (10 in.) blanket of wet snow, and snowshoed down to recover our cache at 3800 metres (12,500 ft.). It was a relatively easy day, but I was now feeling the effects of our rapid ascent. I had a constant pounding headache, and I felt nauseated at night. It seemed that I was now the weakest member of the team, and I began to worry that my weakness would prevent Tom from making the summit too. I began taking a daily ration of 250 milligrams of Diamox, a medication reported to forestall altitude sickness. I silently wondered if I would have the strength for the next few days. The summit was still several kilometres away and 1200 metres (4000 ft.) above us. Allen Carpé called the camp at King Col "one of our most enjoyable camps...a thoroughly comfortable place," but to me it seemed hostile and disquieting. Looming above us was "the headwall," a steep 460 metre-high (1500 ft.) incline that many consider to be the crux of the route.

That evening, each little group retired to its own tent as usual. Later, Warren approached Tom and me. "What would you do if someone fell into a crevasse?" he challenged. "What would you do?" He walked away without waiting for an answer. Tom and I were stunned. We had taken an ice crevasse rescue course at Mount Rainier, and practised the techniques at base camp on Mount McKinley. Still, it was obvious that we weren't as prepared as The

Three Musketeers, who had brought pulleys, snow flukes and other devices useful in crevasse rescue. This failure on our part had apparently been festering in The Three Musketeers' tent, and Warren had either been nominated or had volunteered to express the group's disapproval. I was upset. Climbing this mountain would be hard enough without dissension in the ranks.

The next day, June 9, the heavy snow seemed to be consolidated, and we decided to make a carry up the headwall. Ihor, bounding with enthusiasm and energy, began cutting switchbacks up the steep headwall in snowshoes. Soon after starting, I realized I was in trouble. My legs felt like lead and my back ached with the heavy load. How ironic! Only a few days ago I was shaking my head and thinking Jerry would never make it. But today it was I panting and asking for rest, while Jerry appeared strong. The headwall seemed to go on forever. Once over the headwall we wound our way through fantastic seracs, blocks of ice as big as houses slowly and silently advancing to the sea. We crossed a precarious snow bridge over a crevasse hundreds of metres deep. I was in a world of my own, moving on a monstrous treadmill that seemed never to end.

After a brief rest at about 4570 metres (15,000 ft.), Dave Peterson took over the lead. Happy to be in the lead for the first time, and anxious to prove worthy of the task, he led around a huge crevasse and up an icefall. Suddenly, without warning, he disappeared from sight! He had broken through a thin snow bridge and dropped into the bowels of the icy giant. Warren Grill, who was second on the rope, was jerked forward and dragged by the force of the fall. The presence of the crevasse was betrayed only by a small hole where Dave had punched through. Back on my treadmill, my oxygen-starved brain couldn't grasp what had just happened. I was exhausted to the limit. I sensed activity and saw Ihor running up the hill. I remember wondering "How can he possibly run uphill?" When my brain finally grasped what had taken place, I was simply too weak to help. Fortunately, Ihor and Jeff were much stronger, and took charge of the rescue effort.

Dave's first recollection was the icy walls of the crevasse racing past his face. When he finally came to a stop, he was hanging six metres (20 ft.) down inside a narrow icy slot barely one metre (3 ft.) wide. If he had fallen much farther, he might have wedged hopelessly into the narrow fissure. Fortunately, he had decided to put his entire load in his pack that day. If he had been dragging a heavy sled, it surely would have come crashing down on his head. On the down side, he had opted to wear his snowshoes instead of crampons, making it impossible to simply climb up the walls of the crevasse. The only light in the crevasse came from the tiny hole he had punched through, which bathed the slot in an eerie blue-gray glow.

Jeff's face appeared above, and after collecting his thoughts, Dave set about preparing to ascend the rope. It was not an easy task. First he had to take off his pack and have it hauled up from above. Next he had to remove his snowshoes and organize his prussik knots, which allow a climber to ascend a fixed rope. It was a full half an hour before Dave, shivering and clearly shaken from the fall, at last climbed uninjured from the icy vault. This event would haunt Dave for the rest of the climb. More than once he would pause at the edge of a crevasse and wrestle with fear before crossing.

It was another hour before we were all safely across the crevasse and once again heading uphill. It is a tribute to the group, but especially to Dave, that this near tragedy did not shake us from our plan. We continued up to make a cache at a small campsite at 4730 metres (15,500 ft.), all except Ihor and Mauro, who decided without discussion to make camp near the crevasse. Heading downhill only helped me a little, and I was weak from fatigue when we finally dragged into King Col camp that evening. I privately wondered whether I could possibly achieve the summit, still so far above us.

The next day, June 10, was equally hard, an ambitious push to move camp 760 metres (2500 ft.) from King Col up to the Football Field at 4880 metres (16,000 ft.). The monstrous treadmill continued step after step, hour after weary hour. On the way we were passed by a jovial Pat Morrow and his team, who had successfully collected GPS data that would fix the exact altitude of the highest point in Canada, and were now headed down. They reported hard bulletproof ice and bitterly cold conditions on the plateau, then skied happily down the slope. How I envied them as I turned back up the treadmill. We were now the highest persons on the mountain, and probably in all of Canada.

Finally the roped team of Bennetts and Wageners crested an icefall, reached Football Field camp and began to dig out a campsite. Soon The Three Musketeers arrived, bitterly angry. "How come you went so far?" they demanded. "This is a terrible place to camp!" Their rage took me by surprise, as we had only done exactly what was planned. These divisions, which continued throughout the climb, were the only stains on what would otherwise be a triumphant expedition.

The next day dawned fair and we easily retrieved our cache of supplies from 4730 metres (15,500 ft.). I was feeling a little revived. We planned to make a carry up 370 metres (1200 ft.) to Camp V, aptly named Windy camp by Allen Carpé. As we climbed higher, the weather took a turn for the worse, and an icy wind blew in from the east. The gale stung our faces. My feet grew cold, and I was losing feeling in my left hand. Each man dealt with the cold alone and in icy silence. The final slope to Windy camp seemed to go on forever. Finally we arrived and dropped our loads. Windy camp was an exposed and dreadful place. All the new snow had been blown away and there was only hard ice to pitch tents on. We headed stoically down for another night at the Football Field.

The following day, June 12, we moved our tents up to Windy camp, a gain of only 370 metres (1200 ft.), but it was hard. The weather did not improve. Ihor and Mauro had rejoined us, and we were all together again, nine for the summit. My condition continued to deteriorate. I increased my daily Diamox dosage to 500 milligrams, and spent a restless night with stomach cramps and nausea. I was again tormented by the thought that my weakness would deprive Tom of his shot at the summit.

The next day the weather was unsettled, but we made a carry of 300 metres (1000 ft.) in deteriorating weather to Iona Col, the gateway to Mount Logan's ice plateau. Dave, still haunted by his fall into the crevasse, could not force himself to cross a small snow bridge, and The Three Musketeers had to stash their gear 60 metres (197 ft.) lower. Back at Windy camp, the bitter wind forced us into our tents early. That night the radio call brought bad news. Two climbers on the East Ridge of Mount Logan had fallen. One had a broken leg, and the other a possible concussion. Most of the evening radio chatter was taken up with rescue plans, but there was nothing we could do to help. The East Ridge of Mount Logan was several kilometres away and for us they might as well have been on the moon.

We awoke June 14 to the sound of our tents whipping in a gale as the storm intensified, and we took our first rest day on the mountain. It was a welcome relief for all.

Back home, Mary Fran was having problems of her own. I had given her the task of phoning our pilot, Andy Williams, on a regular basis. In theory it was to work like this: We would be in daily radio contact with Andy Williams. Mary Fran would phone Andy and receive updates on our progress up the mountain. She would then phone a few friends and relatives, as well as Brian Albrecht of the *Cleveland Plain Dealer*. Brian was running a serial piece in the newspaper on the expedition's progress and whereabouts. But the plan fell apart when Andy's vocabulary seemed to be limited to "Yep" and "Nope." Mary Fran could have had better conversations with cheese, which didn't help with the stress level back home.

The next morning the storm abated, and we moved up to our cache at the col, packed the sleds, and finally moved out onto Mount Logan's famous ice plateau, called "that terrible ice cap" by Allen Carpé. What a strange sight it was to see such a plateau, 80 square kilometres (30 sq. mi.), all over 4880 metres (16,000 ft.) above sea level! It was our plan to press on across the plateau as far as we could manage and place our camp as close to the summit as possible. We passed a rocky buttress on the right and headed toward the west summit. Here I was again overcome by fatigue, and had to rest often. Far ahead we saw what looked like an old campsite, but when we arrived it was nothing but strange ice mushrooms carved out by the relentless wind. Here, at about 5370 metres (17,600 ft.), and still 6.5 kilometres (4 mi.) distant from the true summit, we made our Plateau camp on June 15. I was debilitated.

The next three days were all alike. Each morning dawned hopeful, then an ominous lenticular cloud would form over the west peak. Lenticular clouds, which Bradford Washington called "Lenticulus Son-of-a-Bitchus," portend evil weather in the mountains. Sometimes the clouds over Mount Logan were double or even triple lenticular. The storms would move rapidly down the peak, enveloping our little campsite and threatening to destroy it. The constant howling of the wind was usually broken only by the sound of Jerry spattering the snow. Jerry had somehow picked up a nasty case of diarrhea, and could be seen outside at all hours of the day or night exposing tender

Traversing the west peak of Mount Logan with the first view of the true summit across the summit plateau.

Climbers ascending the summit ridge with the east summit behind.

flesh to the elements. These were the hardest days when we were within striking distance of the summit, but were unable to attempt it. At times the ice plateau seemed like a prison from which we would never escape.

One day out of frustration Tom and I decided to take a hike up to a rocky ridge rising above our campsite. When we reached the rocks, we had lost sight of the tents, and I was worried about losing our way. I had taken careful compass readings on the way up, but my brain was not working very well and I even had trouble subtracting 180° to get the compass heading down. I looked at my feet and saw a wayward sparrow, frozen stiff on the ice. "What in the world is he doing up here?" I wondered. "What on earth could have persuaded him to leave the comforts below and come to such a cruel, hostile place." I had no satisfactory answer. Fortunately, the storm cleared a little and we were able to make our way back to the safety of the tents.

Finally, June 19 dawned clear. This was to be our summit day, and we set out in the bitter morning cold at 9:00 am. There was excitement in the air. We all knew that with supplies running low we would probably get only one shot at the summit, and that the next few hours would determine the outcome. We headed up toward the double peak of the west summit, then at about 5490 metres (18,000 ft.) we cached our snowshoes and headed on a traverse across the north side of the west peak. The grade was not very steep, but a fall on the icy slope could have brought serious consequences. Along the way Tom's crampons would not stay on his overboots, and he had to stop and struggle to secure them. This was the first time during the climb that he had put crampons on his overboots, and Jeff was openly angry with him for the delay. Tom finally gave up and went on without the overboots, a very serious decision under such bitterly cold conditions.

After the long traverse, and after cresting a small rise, there it was at last: the true summit of Mount Logan. It was an exciting sight after a 17-day struggle! A long walk to the col between the true summit and the west peak and we were at the foot of the north face.

Based on the topographic map, we had planned to circle around and ascend the gentler East Ridge. But the face did not look too steep, and we decided to traverse it in order to reach a shallow notch just east of the summit. Jeff led the way.

After reaching the notch without difficulty, we took a rest. The summit of Mount Logan, the object of all our ambitions, was now only a few metres away. Tom came up stamping his feet. He had lost all feeling in his toes and was afraid that his feet were freezing. Although the sky was clear, the weather was bitterly cold, and I too was very concerned about the condition of Tom's toes. On the other hand, I had none of the problems that had plagued me going up the headwall or up to Plateau camp. I felt fit and eager! Perhaps it was a rush of adrenaline, or perhaps because of the three days' rest, but on this day I felt as though I could climb forever!

The final ridge to the summit proved to be the most difficult climbing of the route. It was hard ice, and very steep in places. A slip here and one could

Tom Bennett stepping onto the summit, June 19, 1992.

Jerry Wagener and Tom Bennett on the final section of the summit ridge.

tumble hundreds of metres. Jeff cut steps up the final steep step and belayed everyone up. A few more steps and the summit was ours! I turned and watched Tom come up. It was a fantastic sight with rank after rank of unnamed and unclimbed mountains stretching beyond him to the horizon. What a joy it must have been for Tom after his bitter failure on Denali two years before. We embraced each other and wept like babies. Any questions I had as to why I climb were answered in that moment.

Now we could take in the breathtaking panorama. To the south, beyond the massive Mount Saint Elias, was the immense Hubbard Glacier, as big as the state of Rhode Island, pressing relentlessly toward the sea. Farther south was the blue Gulf of Alaska. To the north, the desolate glaciers and mountains of the Wrangle-Saint Elias Range seemed to go on without end. The views to the east and west were obstructed by the east and west summits of Mount Logan, spectacular peaks in their own right. Finally Ihor and Mauro came up and all nine of our motley crew stood on the tiny platform at the top of Canada. We remained on the summit about 40 minutes, congratulating each other and taking the usual pictures, and then it was time to descend. We were still a long way from the safety of our tents, and we knew all too well what Mount Logan could do to the unwary climber.

Our descent to the notch and down across the north face went well. It was not until the traverse of the west peak that I became aware of how tired Jerry was. He walked as if in a trance. Twice he simply fell over, toppling like a toy soldier. Fortunately, each time he fell, we held. I was glad when we were finally off the icy slope of the west peak. As soon as we were beyond the steep traverse, Tom unroped and made a dash for the relative warmth of the tent and his sleeping bag. He had long ago lost any feeling in his feet and was frightened that his toes were frostbitten. We returned to our tents at 11:00 pm after a 14-hour summit day, and turned in exhausted yet overjoyed by our success.

The next morning I was relieved to see that Tom's toes were bright pink, with none of the blisters that forecast frostbite damage. Jerry was not so lucky. After returning to the tent, three of his fingers began to blister, and would later turn black from frostbite. I was alarmed. None of us had experienced deep frostbite before, and we were still several days away from medical treatment.

The next day, June 20, dawned unsettled. The familiar lenticular cloud formed over the west peak early in the day forecasting bad weather, but sun and clouds kept playing throughout the morning. I was desperate to escape from the icy plateau, but Jeff was reluctant to move. After noon the weather seemed to clear and some of the surrounding peaks came into view. I begged Jeff to pack up and go, and at last he relented. We quickly took down the tents, packed up and started toward Iona Col with Tom in the lead. But after only a few minutes I could see that we had made a mistake. A brutal blizzard blew up so fierce that Tom could not follow the thin line of wands leading to safety. At times I completely lost sight of him at the end of the rope. Still we struggled on. Our situation was turning desperate. One of my ears froze where it was exposed below my hat. Finally Ihor came running up from behind and screamed above the howling gale, "The Musketeers want to go back!" There was no discussion necessary. We immediately wheeled in our tracks and started a desperate march back toward Plateau camp. Once there, we had to make camp in the worst possible conditions, with the ruthless wind threatening to snatch the tents and blow them away forever. We were sternly punished for our bad decision, and I felt personally responsible. There was no talk of moving for the rest of the day.

Late that same evening the skies cleared, though it was still bitterly cold. I looked out of the tent and was amazed to see Ihor and Mauro packing up! "Well, we're off. See you later!" said Ihor cheerfully. A few others also wanted to go down with Ihor and Mauro, but I would have none of it. I was shaken by the events earlier in the day, and felt that to descend at night, when temperatures often reached -40° on the plateau, was foolhardy. We watched Ihor and Mauro disappear across the plateau, and crawled back into our bags.

The next day the weather looked better, so we hurriedly packed up and headed off in Ihor's tracks. The weather held that morning, but unfortunately, blindly following Ihor's tracks was not a wise choice. Ihor missed the proper col to get off the plateau, heading much too far to the west, and so did we. As a result we had to negotiate a steep ice slope to get off the plateau. It was a nerve-wracking business, and I was in no mood to deal with such mistakes. I fell on the icy traverse, and though the rope held me, I was frustrated and exhausted.

Back on track, we packed down to Windy camp where we again found Ihor and Mauro, who had stopped there after their nighttime descent. Another expedition was also at Windy camp, on its way up. But they were already exhausted, and one member was sick from the altitude. They had given up.

After a brief rest, we continued toward King Col. The route was now very different from the last time we had seen it. Only a few centimetres of our wands were visible above the snow, and we floundered in the deep powder. At one point Jerry lost his balance, fell off his snowshoes, and disappeared instantly into the fluff. His attempts to push himself upright with his ski poles were futile, as the poles also disappeared into the bottomless powder. Jerry floundered for several minutes before he finally managed to regain his feet. All the way down, King Peak dramatically appeared and disappeared in the chaotic storm clouds. Snow fell heavily. Finally at the top of the headwall, we hesitated, not knowing if the slope was ripe for avalanche. But Tom and I simply unroped and pushed our sleds down. We followed, despite Jeff's protests, sliding down in the tracks left by the sleds. We were simply too spent to do anything else. Once the slope had been tested, everyone else followed in kind. Safely down at King Col, we made camp for the night, having descended 1220 metres (4000 ft.) from Plateau camp in eight kilometres (5 mi.).

The storm raged on all the next day and we remained at King Col camp.

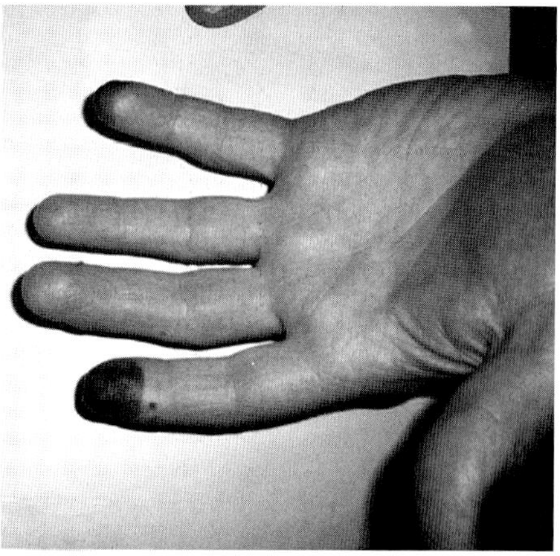

Jerry Wagener's frostbitten fingers. Photo Jeff Wagener.

We packed up June 23 and headed down from the col, hoping to fly out that same day. We had been in radio contact with Andy Williams, and had requested a fly-out from King Trench camp at 3350 metres (11,000 ft.), especially for Jerry, whose frostbitten fingers had now turned an ominous black. We wallowed through deep snow down to King Trench camp, and tried to radio Andy, as arranged, at 10:00 am. The flying weather was perfect, but Andy apparently wasn't listening. Throughout our climb Andy Williams had seemed a little too casual, and this day was no exception. So we pressed on to the standard landing site on the Quintino-Sella Glacier at 2740 metres (9000 ft.).

We still couldn't reach Andy on the radio, but another pilot appeared from nowhere and landed. He promised to contact Andy for us, then disappeared. Eventually the little red Cessna of Icefield Ranges Expeditions did appear, and Andy flew Jerry and Jeff Wagener off the glacier before nightfall. Tom and I followed the next morning, followed in turn by Dave Peterson. Then, amazingly, but true to form, Andy flew off to do a lucrative grizzly bear survey, leaving Warren and Greg to spend another cold night on the glacier!

Back at Kluane Lake, we revelled in the sights, sounds and smells of spring in the Yukon. Fields of lupine bloomed everywhere, and for the first time in 23 days we felt warm breezes on our skin. Perhaps one cannot fully appreciate the joy of simple pleasures without enduring hardship.

And so all ended well. Our expedition enjoyed remarkable success, and Jerry's fingers did not have to be amputated. Mount Logan will always have my utmost respect, however. The weather, together with the isolation, makes an ascent by any route a serious undertaking. From the point of view of total effort, it is certainly the most demanding of all the Canadian highpoints.

This was the springboard I needed for the Canadian highpoints, and I quietly promised myself to complete the entire project. I felt that surely all the other highpoints would be easy by comparison. Little did I realize what hardship and misfortune awaited us in the Northwest Territories!

Campsite in the sanctuary north of Mount Nirvana.

Mount Nirvana, Mountain of Mystery

Long have I waited lonely,
shunned as a thing accursed,
Monstrous, moody, pathetic,
the last of the lands and the first....

When Tom and I returned from our ordeal on Mount Logan in 1992, we were beat. Brian Albrecht, writing a follow-up article for the *Cleveland Plain Dealer*, said I looked as if I had been "mugged by a mountain." My face was flaming red from high-altitude sunburn, my ears were scaling from frostbite, and my toes were sore. I hobbled for days from the lingering toe-tenderness called "boot bang," caused by the repeated slamming of toes against boots during the descent. I was seven kilograms (15 lbs.) lighter than before we left, and my whole body ached.

"Hey Tom, why don't we do something easy next year? Something fun!"

"How about the Northwest Territories?" he suggested. "There's nothing up there over 3000 metres (9843 ft.); should be a walk in the park."

A quick trip to the local library seemed to confirm the logic. The highest point in the Northwest Territories was listed as Mount Sir James McBrian at 2760 metres (9055 ft.), and nearly every atlas and encyclopedia on the shelf verified this. Mount Sir James McBrian, located deep in the Ragged Range of the Logan Mountains, is one of several peaks known collectively as "The Cirque of the Unclimbables." This group of peaks is famous among technical rock jocks for its 1000-metre (3000 ft.) vertical faces with perfect vertical cracks, especially on the imposing spire known as the "Lotus Flower Tower." But despite this rather ominous reputation, Mount Sir James McBrian is not difficult to access or to climb. We figured that a flight to remote Glacier Lake, a one-day approach, and a one-day climb ought to do it. No problem, right? I thought it might be fun to have some company on this climb, so I put a note in the Highpointers Club newsletter for anyone interested in joining us.

But just a few months before we were scheduled to leave, I received some stunning news. Two members of the Highpointers Club wrote to tell me that the highest point of the Northwest Territories was *not* Mount Sir James McBrian, but was actually a mysterious mountain 32 kilometres (20 mi.) farther south called Mount Nirvana. A careful check of Canadian topographic maps confirmed that Mount Nirvana, at 2773 metres (9097 ft.), was 13 metres (43 ft.) higher. Our plans were thrown into disarray. We knew nothing about this new mountain. How could we approach it and climb it? How hard was it? What did it look like? I could find no pictures, and written accounts were scarce, so I turned to the American Alpine Club library for help.

Soon three *American Alpine Journal* articles arrived. The late Bill Buckingham and Lew Surdam had first climbed Mount Nirvana in 1965. They had landed at remote Lonely Lake and made their way over a tangle of intervening peaks and passes to reach the mountain. But after seeing the incredible turrets and ramparts of its east and southern flanks, they had decided Nirvana was more of an undertaking than they were prepared for. They circled around to the north face where they found a weakness, and made the first ascent up a difficult mixture of rock and ice. Andrew Embick and two companions made a second ascent from the north in 1975. Apparently, Mount Nirvana had not been climbed in 18 years.

After looking at the map, I reasoned that the north face of Mount Nirvana could be reached by landing on Rabbitkettle Lake and then hiking about 29 kilometres (18 mi.) up the Rabbitkettle River. This, in fact, was the only sensible route to the north side without resorting to a helicopter landing. I felt we had to try the north face as I was not sure that any other route would be possible. Although nervous about the climb, I felt the approach would be easy. I pictured myself strolling through grassy meadows along the riverbank, or perhaps through lovely conifer forest, stopping to catch our limit of trout for dinner. Little did I know what misery awaited us along the banks of the Rabbitkettle River.

A party of four was recruited for the adventure: Tom, me, our friend Joe Elliott and Bob Anderson, a highpointer from Massachusetts. We could fly to Rabbitkettle Lake from Fort Liard, Northwest Territories, or Watson Lake in the Yukon. But a commercial flight from Ohio to Watson Lake was almost $900 per person—pretty expensive for a low budget expedition. I started looking around for cheaper alternatives. Just as my travel agent was beginning to lose patience, she found that we could fly to Edmonton, Alberta, for only $380. We could then rent a full-size car, and if we could stuff in four people plus gear and supplies and drive 1300 kilometres (800 mi.) up the Alaska Highway, we'd be dollars ahead! Sure enough, by making use of every inch of space and lashing duffel bags on the trunk, we made it. Every couple of hours we had to pry ourselves out of our cramped little holes just to stretch.

I enjoyed this trip. We were able to see the Alaska Highway, an acclaimed engineering marvel built during World War II, from Dawson Creek to Fort

Nelson. Once in Fort Nelson we turned north for 240 tedious kilometres (150 mi.) on gravel road to Fort Liard. There we met Rob Borelli, the pilot and general manager for Deh Cho Air.

The plan called for Deh Cho Air to circle Mount Nirvana, airdrop 54 kilograms (120 lbs.) of food and supplies at the foot of the mountain, then land us at Rabbitkettle Lake. Our schedule allowed two days for the approach, five days at Nirvana, and two days out. No problem. But that's where everything that could possibly go wrong went wrong.

First, the DeHaviland Otter, which Deh Cho Air uses to fly to Rabbitkettle Lake, landed streaked with oil behind the engine cowling. The pilot, Rob Borelli, muttered "If this damn thing isn't leaking oil, then it's empty!" But this was clearly more than a routine leak. The engine had cracked a cylinder, and it took all the next day to repair. Our time at Nirvana had been cut to four days. Then, just when it looked as if the repair was going badly, Rob announced "Fixed! Be at the dock ready to go in 20 minutes." Total chaos ensued as we rushed to throw gear and supplies into packs and bags.

Once we were in the air, our situation looked grim. As we approached Mount Nirvana, the weather turned ominous. We could see almost nothing except thick black clouds, and an occasional ugly jagged peak flying by. It occurred to me that we might die before even reaching the mountain! After flying nearly blind through the ragged mountains, Rob finally shook his head and turned back. There would be no airdrop this day. Rob pointed to the Rabbitkettle River winding through the mist below, "I'm sure glad it's you going down there and not me." My vision of strolling along the riverbank was shattered! Below us stretched an endless maze of bogs and dense alderbrush (or Velcro, as the locals affectionately called it). We were about to get a very nasty lesson about bushwhacking in the near Arctic.

Rabbitkettle Lake is in Nahanni National Park, and when we landed we found a lonely warden station manned by two lonely wardens. Quizzing the wardens didn't do a thing for our confidence.

"Ever hear of anyone going up the Rabbitkettle River?" I asked.

"Nope. Why would anyone want to do that?"

"We're going to climb Mount Nirvana," I explained. "It's the highest mountain in the Northwest Territories!"

"Good luck," came the dry reply. "You're going to need it."

The wardens took us to the river and helped us cross an old hand-operated ferry to the other side. First they showed us the travertine terraces and pools of the Rabbitkettle Hot Springs. They looked like a miniature Mammoth Hot Springs, somehow displaced from Yellowstone Park. The wardens then pointed us into the brush. There was no trail. The first eight kilometres (5 mi.) up the Rabbitkettle River were a nightmare. Sometimes slogging deep in mud, sometimes pressing through dense brush, and always surrounded by clouds of mosquitoes, we took eight hours to bushwhack the eight kilometres (5 mi.). Rain drizzled on and off throughout the day, adding to our already gloomy moods.

We finally staggered onto a gravel bar to pitch camp the first night. We were all in a state of weary shock. I privately wondered how we could possibly cover the remaining 21 kilometres (13 mi.) to Mount Nirvana's north face and still have enough energy left for a summit attempt. But once we had made camp and had supper, things looked a little brighter. Maybe the terrain would improve tomorrow. It certainly couldn't get any worse! Then I discovered a shocking setback.

"Hey, who's got the food bags marked four through 10?"

"Not me."

"Nope."

Suddenly things had become worse, *much* worse! In our haste to pack up and leave, I had left behind seven days' worth of food on the dock in Fort Liard. My face flushed. How could I have been so careless? The food was my responsibility, and this single neglectful act had now jeopardized the entire expedition. This would be the subject of a lot of good-natured ridicule later, but at the time it was anything but funny. After a brief council, we decided to ration the food and continue. We had only two days' worth of food to last the seven arduous days ahead. We decided to cache as much gear as we could to lighten our loads, including our rope ascenders, a decision that we would later regret.

The next day we were able to follow a few game trails, but it still took us 10 hours to travel 21 rugged kilometres (13 mi.). The going was tough. Near the end of the day Tom and I were waiting for Joe and Bob to catch up. After 15 minutes Joe came dragging in alone and said, "Bob turned back. He's had enough." I thought briefly about going after him. Perhaps I could make him change his mind. But then it occurred to me that he might be the only one doing the sensible thing. We pressed on and camped on a sandbar by the river.

In the morning we discovered we'd had a piece of luck. A grizzly bear had passed in front of our tent during the night, leaving gigantic footprints in the sand. The beast had lumbered only two metres (6 ft.) from our tent, but had, to our relief, left us alone.

Just when we thought the terrain couldn't possibly get worse, it did. The final eight kilometres (5mi.), during which we gained 1160 metres (3800 ft.) in elevation, were like a bad dream. There were enormous boulder fields covered with several centimetres of thick reindeer moss. Often one of us would step on what looked like secure footing, only to have a foot plunge into a fissure between two boulders. The brush was so thick it seemed nearly impossible to penetrate. It took us a full 12 hours to cover the last eight kilometres (5 mi.), and we finally staggered to the top of a waterfall in dense fog. It was 11:00 pm, July 18, 1993. Mount Nirvana was just in front of us, but still we hadn't seen it. Just then, the fog began to lift, revealing a spectacular and monstrous landscape in the waning arctic light. To our left and right vertical walls climbed 900 metres (3000 ft.) into the mist. A sanctuary few people had ever seen, a truly unspoiled Yosemite, encircled us. Finally, Nirvana itself came into view. Its appearance did nothing for our confidence. It was guarded on the north by an icefall that had formed where the glacier tumbled steeply over a large

The author and Tom Bennett atop the nunatak north of Mount Nirvana.

nunatak, an island of rock in the middle of the advancing ice. Beyond the glacier was a huge bergschrund, or crack, separating the ice from the mountain, and above the bergschrund was a threatening mixture of ice and steep rock. We made camp at the top of the waterfall and went to bed nervous and hungry after sharing a few precious mouthfulls of rice. It rained all the next day. We had only two days left in which to summit Mount Nirvana.

The following day, July 20, dawned fair and we gathered our climbing gear and nervously headed toward the north face of Mount Nirvana. The icefall was fairly easily passed on the left, and after a few roped pitches we reached the top of the nunatak at about 2:00 pm. It was obvious that the climbing would be extremely slow that day as we had three people on two ropes. This meant that only one person could climb at a time. First the lead climber would go up, then the second and finally the third climber would join the other two. If we had not left the ascenders behind, then the third climber could have ascended at the same time the first climber was leading the next pitch.

The bergschrund was a problem. This huge crack between the glacier and the mountain forms because the glacier is inexorably moving down toward the valley. The bergschrund was deep, and in most places overhanging. We finally crossed the 'schrund on the right of the face where an avalanche had created a narrow bridge. Tom led over the bridge and straight up the avalanche chute. He was still climbing when he reached the end of his 46 metre-long (150 ft.) rope, so Joe started climbing behind him. Soon we were all three climbing—unprotected—straight up the avalanche chute, causing Tom a few very tense moments. This manoeuvre was definitely not according to the manual! Snow and expletives rained down upon Joe and me below. Tom finally reached the rock and the climbing became more secure, but was still painfully slow.

Tom and I alternated leads up the face and steadily gained altitude. The rock was surprisingly loose. Several times I reached what looked like a secure handhold only to have it pop off in my hand. This can be a real fright, and never failed to cause my heart to flutter a little.

At 11:00 pm I led to a point on the northwest ridge only about 30 metres (98 ft.) below the top of Nirvana. But the route above was vertical and almost devoid of holds. My heart sank! I felt sure I couldn't climb it. Tom was our best rock climber, so he pressed the climb to a point that appeared to be only about 10 metres (33 ft.) below the summit. At the same time the weather was slowly turning evil. The wind picked up, and snowflakes began to fly. In the face of difficult rock and the worsening weather, Tom came down. We all knew that our safety now depended on a speedy retreat. We also knew at once that we had neither the time nor the energy to mount another summit attempt. We had failed.

We turned our attention to setting up rappels on the north face. It was a painfully slow process. The first person, usually Tom, would rappel down the ropes in the darkness, not really knowing what was at the bottom, then Joe and I would follow. Once we were down we would say a prayer, and pull on the rope. If the rope had jammed at any point, we would have been in very deep trouble, as we had no ascenders with which to climb up. But each rappel worked out, and we slowly descended as night closed in. The storm intensified, and we were soon in the teeth of a raging blizzard.

While standing on one narrow ledge, I was distracted by a peculiar hissing sound. I looked over and was horrified to see an avalanche barrelling down to my right in the strange blue-gray glow of the arctic night. The sight was surreal and terrifying! If we were struck by such an avalanche, would it tear us from the face? We could only guess. At that moment, I was more frightened than I had ever been on a mountain. Here, I reflected, we might indeed encounter our nirvana, "the final release of the soul."

Rappelling down the face of a large mountain is tricky business. You reach a ledge near the end of the ropes where you *must* find a suitable anchor point for the next rappel. At first we were lucky, but eventually we reached a ledge where there was no anchor point: no rock horn on which to place a nylon sling, and no crack in which to place a climbing nut.

"There's nothing here to anchor on," said Tom. "We're screwed!"

"What about this?" I asked. I had managed to dig a small rock out of the ice, and placed it between two other rocks. Although far from recommended procedure, here was our anchor point. Tom and Joe looked at me incredulously and just shook their heads. Would it hold? When it came time to trust our weight, and our lives, to that small rock, I closed my eyes and imagined a body hurtling down the stony face of Mount Nirvana. I pictured its lifeless form glancing off the rocky face, and finally coming to rest on the glacier far below. My mind drifted back to Montana in 1967 when a rappel anchor had broken free, sending me screaming 15 metres (50 ft.) down the rock where I shattered several bones. That mishap was

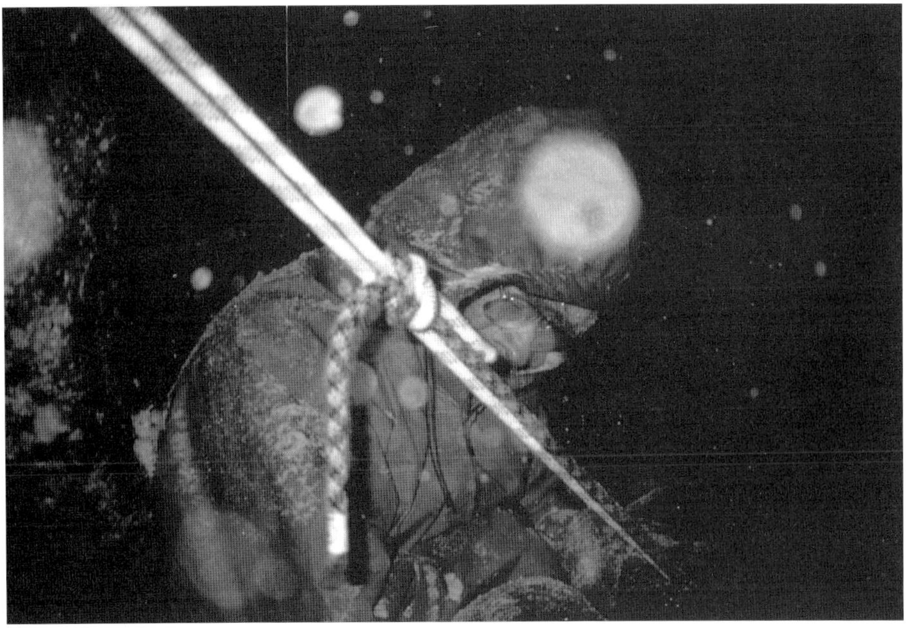

The author rappelling down the north face at night.

followed by surgery and a long recovery in a Bozeman hospital. Survival here would be much more unlikely.

But the night finally ended, and we made our last rappel to land below the bergschrund just as the morning sun kissed the glacier. We silently slumped in the snow and fell asleep.

The trek to Rabbitkettle Lake was no better than it had been coming up. The moss-covered boulders, the bogs, the brush and the mosquitoes had not been figments of our imagination. In fact, they seemed even worse to us in our poor condition. Tired and hungry, we doted over each little bouillon cube and mouthful of rice. The climb had been a learning experience to say the least, and one that would preoccupy my thoughts for the next three years. A failure of this kind does not die easily, and I gnawed on it like a bitter crust day after day. It would be three long years before Tom and I would return, and we would do so armed with a great deal more knowledge and planning.

I had learned that Mount Nirvana, even more than Mount Logan, was the key to the 12 summits of Canada. To complete the project, we had to find a way to climb this forbidding granite pinnacle.

Mount Columbia, and the Prairie Provinces

But the stars throng out in their glory,
And they sing of the God in man;
They sing of the Mighty Master,
Of the loom his fingers span,
Where a star or a soul is a part of the whole,
And weft in the wondrous plan.

Our bitter failure on Mount Nirvana in 1993 had left me disappointed and full of doubt. Suddenly not all things were possible. Should I continue to climb the Canadian highpoints knowing that in order to complete the project I would someday have to return to Mount Nirvana? I decided to try something less ambitious in 1994, but at the same time I knew we needed a challenge to build our confidence. Mount Columbia, the highpoint of Alberta, seemed to fill the bill. At 3747 metres (12,296 ft.), Mount Columbia is a jewel of the Canadian Rockies. It is not a technically difficult climb, and lies only a few kilometres from the Icefields Parkway, the main road between Banff and Jasper. But Mount Columbia is no pushover either. It sits high atop the Columbia Icefield and is guarded by heavily crevassed glaciers on all sides. The icefield and surrounding peaks receive a huge amount of precipitation every year, and good weather seldom lasts long.

One of Tom's friends, Brian Butler, expressed an interest in coming with us, which made our group a threesome. Brian had never climbed a mountain before, but he was an accomplished cyclist, and was strong and determined. He was also willing to drive and share expenses, so the plan was born.

Brian, Tom and I would pile into Brian's VW Passat and drive to Manitoba where we would "climb" Manitoba's highpoint, Baldy Mountain. From there we would continue west to the Cypress Hills of Saskatchewan, then on to Calgary, Alberta. In Calgary we would meet Mary Fran and Jenny at the airport, pick up a rental car, and all drive to Lake Louise in Banff National Park. Mary Fran and Jenny planned to sightsee in Jasper National Park while we climbed Mount Columbia. It all seemed to fit together rather well: a combination climbing trip and family vacation.

Manitoba

Our climb of Baldy Mountain began about 7:00 pm, the evening of July 11, 1994. Tom, Brian Butler and I had already driven 1120 kilometres (700 mi.) that day and we were weary of watching the vast Canadian prairies go by. The beautiful forested hills of Riding Mountain and Duck Mountain provincial parks provided a welcome relief. Lovely, secluded lakes dotted the hills, and wildlife was plentiful.

We turned north on Highway 366 from Grandview, Manitoba, and drove toward threatening clouds hovering over Baldy Mountain. The road was well maintained, and the drive uneventful, except for our spotting a coyote and a few deer. After 35 kilometres (22 mi.) we turned left, and pulled into the parking lot at the summit of Baldy Mountain. A wooden lookout tower crowns the summit. This is not the sort of highpoint that a climber would go to for any reason other than to complete a list. The following tongue-in-cheek account is from my journal entry for that day:

"The long 46 metre (150 ft.) approach to the lookout tower was tiring, but uneventful. It was then that we received our first sight of the imposing tower. The lower level looked straightforward, but the upper section was dark and intimidating, its gnarly head rising well above the treetops. But there was no turning back now...I could concentrate only on the path before me: two steps and rest, two steps and rest.... The top seemed so near; only a few steps above us. Finally I struggled to the summit platform, and there was nowhere left to climb. The plains of Manitoba stretched away below us to the horizon. We embraced, and were overwhelmed by the moment."

Tom Bennett on the lookout tower on top of Baldy Mountain.

Brian Butler and Tom Bennett on the "summit" of the Cypress Hills, highpoint of Saskatchewan.

After a few minutes on top it started to rain. We returned to the car and headed west toward Saskatchewan.

Saskatchewan

It was in Saskatchewan that Brian Butler began to regret his offer to drive. We carefully followed Highway 271 southwest of Maple Creek, then on a series of ever-smaller roads leading toward the top of the Cypress Hills. As we neared the top of the hill, the wet road became very gooey. Brian kept going, mainly because he had no choice. To stop was to stop permanently! The road showed no improvement along the top of the hill, and our poor VW wallowed constantly left and right. The cattle on the open range seemed oblivious to our dilemma, and were very reluctant to get out of our way. Finally we found the little road that led to the highpoint from the north, and gave a whole new meaning to the word "road." It was practically nonexistent. At last we arrived at the sacred spot and came to a reluctant halt.

I have never, I mean *never*, seen a flatter highpoint, hands down, and that includes Iowa, Indiana and Kansas! The land stretched over a kilometre from north to south without changing more than five metres in elevation. Tom, Brian Butler and I dutifully climbed the fence and paced off about 100 metres (328 ft.) south to the spot marked "4567 ft." on our topographic map. But was it really the highest point? I had no idea. Nonetheless, we took the obligatory pictures, then headed back to the VW.

After a couple of tense moments getting the car turned around on the mushy road, we careened back down the hill, always on the verge of getting hopelessly stuck. All the way back to Maple Creek the poor VW emitted pitiful grinding noises. In Maple Creek we pulled into a car wash, raised the hood, and spent a small fortune in "loonies" washing the caked mud off the engine. We all agreed we had been very lucky that time.

Alberta

The 4:00 am wake-up call roused Tom, Brian and me from a sound sleep in the Lake Louise Inn. It was July 14, 1994. We had packed the night before, and so, after waving goodbye to Mary Fran and Jenny, we were soon headed north on Alberta Highway 93, the Icefields Parkway. The sky was crystal clear, revealing the mountains with snowfields glowing pink in the early morning light. We arrived at the turn-off to the Athabasca Glacier at about 6:00 am and drove through the gate to the climbers' parking lot at 2040 metres (6700 ft.). Unfortunately, it was not possible to take the snowcoach onto the Athabasca Glacier, or to drive any farther up the road as a second gate blocked the way. This left the approach rather longer than I had planned.

But full of optimism, we quickly packed up to the snowcoach parking lot on the glacier at about 2260 metres (7400 ft.). We roped up at the parking lot, even though it hardly seemed necessary, and headed up toward the first icefall. The Athabasca Glacier tumbles down from the Columbia Icefield in three giant steps. The lower two icefalls were hopelessly jumbled in the centre, so it was necessary to choose either the right or left side. The right side looked the easiest, but it was threatened by a hanging glacier, which was already being warmed by the morning sun. The left side was also threatened by a glacier and by rockfall from cliffs above, but it looked like the lesser of two evils, so we chose the left. Hurrying over rock and ice rubble, we easily attained the top of the second icefall, with only a straightforward ramp leading to the Columbia Icefield. Looking down, we wished we had gone up the right side, which looked easier. I was leading at this point, and suddenly dropped up to my waist into a crevasse. Surprised, and giving a shriek, I popped back out. Amazing how one can defy the laws of gravity at such times! The warden had informed us that a tourist, travelling unroped, had died in a crevasse on the Athabasca Glacier only five days earlier.

Tom then took the lead up the ramp and onto the icefield. After stopping for lunch at 1:00 pm, the snow became quite soft. Tom was breaking trail and sinking about 15 centimetres (6 in.), enough to make the going hard, but not enough to justify donning our snowshoes. Each little rise in the icefield looked only a ropelength away, but was actually much farther. Tom did a yeoman's job breaking trail all the way across the icefield. Finally, Mount Columbia appeared over the horizon looking spectacular. Still we slogged on. We were sinking 15-20 centimetres (6-8 in.) with every step, and at last decided to put on snowshoes. The snowshoes helped a lot, but it was still heavy going as I took over the lead. Brian and I were especially spent!

Camp at the trench on the Columbia Icefield east of Mount Columbia with The Twins in the background.

At last, we headed down into the trench, just as the weather turned foul. The sides of the trench were heavily crevassed, and I strained to see the best way down. But the light was so poor I couldn't see through the rain, so we set up camp near the top of the trench in a driving rainstorm. It was 7:00 pm, at least two hours later than I had expected to arrive at the trench.

We hastily set up the tent and dove inside, totally wiped from the approach. We had travelled 13 kilometres (8 mi.), gaining 880 metres (2900 ft.) in elevation, then dropping down about 90 metres (300 ft.). We cooked supper inside the tent, not a practice that I recommend, but one that we usually resort to in bad weather. We were so tired, I was concerned whether we could mount a serious summit attempt the next day. Brian seemed especially tired and couldn't keep supper down, diving for the tent door on one occasion to throw up. We drifted off to sleep early that night.

The next morning we awoke to the sound of rain on the tent fly. I was quietly relieved to see bad weather, as we sorely needed a rest day before the summit attempt. The day continued to be blustery with a strong thunderstorm in the late afternoon, so we spent our second day resting and telling Brian stories of our glorious highpoint climbs of the past. The next morning I awoke to the sound of our watch alarms at 5:00 am, and stuck my nose outside. Fantastic! There was not a cloud in the sky, and the cold night had frozen the wet snow into a surface perfect for cramponing. Excited, we gulped a cold breakfast, roped up and started down into the trench. The crevasses on the sides of the trench were easily bypassed as we descended about 120 metres (400 ft.), then started up the other side. The snow was still hard, and we made good time to the base of Mount Columbia's summit pyramid. Here we cached our snowshoes and started up the steep east face.

The east face of Mount Columbia is about 600 metres (2000 ft.) high, and runs at an angle of 40°-45°. We decided to climb straight up the left side of the face. The snow was turning soft, so it didn't seem worth the trouble to belay. We simply headed up, roped together, with Tom in the lead. After about 300 metres (1000 ft.), I took the lead for the steepest part of the face. By now I was postholeing up the steep slope in deep, wet snow. It was exhausting work, and my glasses quickly fogged over. At the top of the steepest part of the face, I stamped out a platform and brought up Tom and Brian. I was wasted! Tom took over the lead up the top portion of the face, staying on the left side.

Soon, I heard Tom give a whoop! Brian disappeared over the slope above and also gave a yell. Shortly I reached them and had no more to climb. The top came much sooner than I had expected.

Mount Columbia has a double summit, and the summit toward the northwest and about 50 metres (164 ft.) away looked higher. So we dropped down to a little col and scrambled up for our summit celebration. The weather was perfect. Clouds occasionally swept up, blowing fog over the summit from the west, but then they would clear, revealing a breathtaking panorama. Amazing-looking peaks loomed off to the north and west. One we could easily identify was the steep and forbidding Mount Alberta, the last major peak of the Canadian Rockies to be climbed. Mount Alberta was considered unclimbable until it was finally scaled by a Japanese expedition in 1925. The Columbia Glacier, which flows down from the north end of the trench, is especially spectacular from this vantage point. This glacier is readily identified by its striking ogives, periodic bands of dark and light that mark the

The Columbia Glacier from the summit of Mount Columbia showing the ogive bands.

Brian Butler clowning in the tracks of the avalanche the party set off on the descent.

summer and winter advance of the ice. After the usual round of picture taking and laughter, we settled down for a well-earned snack. We were on the summit about 45 glorious minutes.

We again roped up and I headed back down the east face. As soon as I reached the steepest part of the face and planted my foot, the entire east face avalanched! The avalanche rolled 300 metres (1000 ft.) down the face, across a crevasse, and silently spread out on the gentle slope below. I was shocked and a little frightened. I had not realized that the face was so unconsolidated. It was a wet slab avalanche, not as spectacular as the huge avalanches that thunder down north faces from big cornices and ice cliffs, but just as dangerous. Had we been unlucky, we might have had a quick and deadly ride down the mountain.

A slope is supposedly safe immediately after an avalanche, but I was a little shaken, and not so sure. We decided to belay a few pitches down the face with pickets and ice axes to secure the belays. But after five or six pitches we abandoned the belays and simply scurried down, anxious to be off the face and beyond the tracks of the avalanche.

Finally we reached the safety of level ground and our snowshoe cache. Here we unroped, and each climber returned to camp at his own pace, there being no apparent crevasse danger. The two youngsters arrived at camp first, with the old man of the group dragging in about an hour after Brian, who stayed very strong throughout the day. We were all feeling tired, so we settled down to an evening of supper and relaxation. We were eight hours on the ascent, 45 minutes on top, and five hours on our return back to camp. The total elevation gain was 1040 metres (3400 ft.), plus another 100 metres (300 ft.) or so back up the east side of the trench to camp, over a total distance of about 14 kilometres (9 mi.): a very respectable day. We turned in content with the joy of a climb well done.

One disconcerting note: on our return to camp I noticed that the fly of my North Face Oval Intention tent was shredded in several places. High altitude exposure to UV had finally taken its toll, and the embrittled fly had disintegrated as it stretched taut in the hot sun. I mourned the loss of my old reliable North Face tent, which had seen us through so many memorable highpoints of the past. We re-pitched the tent to put the ground plastic between the tent and the fly, an arrangement that actually worked pretty well.

We awoke at 5:00 am the next morning with plans to break camp and move it about three kilometres (1.8 mi.) to 2900 metres (9600 ft.), then climb Snow Dome. Snow Dome is an easy climb, but a very unique one. Its summit is the triple divide point for North America, the point from which water flows to three oceans: the Atlantic, Pacific and Arctic. But the sound of rain on the fly again stalled our plans, and we stayed at the trench until 1:00 pm. The weather broke a little and we headed back across the icefield. It was not a pleasant march as we trudged through soft snow and intermittent rain showers. Finally, we made camp at the top of the Athabasca Glacier at 4:30 pm.

It was still raining, so we engaged in our usual poor practice of cooking in the tent. Unfortunately, Tom had a bad habit of overpriming our Whisperlite stove. On this occasion he outdid himself, and the stove, together with his foam pad, burst into flames. Time to panic! Brian tried to beat the flames out with his hand, a decidedly bad idea that set his hand on fire! I ended the crisis by throwing the stove and flaming foam pad into the snow. After realizing that no one was hurt and no damage was done, the entire event became hysterically funny and we rolled inside the tent laughing. It was actually a dangerous event, which could have cost us the tent.

The next day we roped up at 7:30 am, and descended the Athabasca Glacier on the right side (looking up). This turned out to be much easier than the left, and we arrived at the snowcoach parking lot at about 10:00 am. We felt like animals in a zoo as we walked down the road to the climbers' parking lot. Hundreds of tourists pointed and waved, and a throng of Japanese clicked camera shutters in rapid-fire. Tom and Brian registered our return at the warden station, and I was glad to find Mary Fran and Jenny waiting for me in the parking lot.

It was a good climb and a great summit. The climb is comparable to Mount Rainier, Washington, both in total effort and in technical difficulty. Soft snow and mixed weather presented the greatest hardships, but all considered, it was a very satisfying summit.

We felt especially lucky when a national park warden told us that he had tried to climb Mount Columbia three times, only to be beaten back by bad weather each time.

The rest of the trip we spent being tourists, although we took time out to climb Mount Temple and do a little rock climbing. Mary Fran and Jenny headed home, courtesy of American Airlines, while Brian, Tom and I drudged back across the prairies by Volkswagon.

Mount Fairweather, Kingdom of Snow

You who this faint day the High North is luring
Unto her vastness, taintlessly sweet;
You who are steel-braced, straight-lipped, enduring,
Dreadless in danger and dire in defeat:
Honor the High North ever and ever,
Whether she crown you, or whether she slay;
Suffer her fury, cherish and love her—
He who would rule, he must learn to obey.

I was relieved to see Dan and Tom waiting for me when I arrived at the little airport in Yakutat, Alaska, on Saturday, June 10, 1995. We had taken different routes to get there in order to use a hodgepodge of frequent flyer miles. I had first taken Mary Fran and Jenny on a family vacation to Denali National Park, put them on the Regent Star cruise ship bound for Vancouver, then caught the southbound flight from Anchorage to Yakutat. Dan and Tom had taken a United Airline flight through Seattle, arriving in Yakutat on the morning northbound flight. There was a lot of potential for things to go amiss, yet here we were right on schedule. We walked over to the Gulf Air hanger and began the tedious chore of sorting and packing gear for the climb.

As usual at the start of a big climb, I was apprehensive. What hardship or fortune awaited us on the icy slopes of Mount Fairweather? Our failure on Mount Nirvana two years before had taught me a new respect for high places, and I no longer assumed success would be the outcome. Nearly three years before, from the summit of Mount Logan, we had seen a "shining mountain of promise" far to the southeast; a beautiful pyramid standing head and shoulders above its neighbours. I pointed to Mount Fairweather and announced that we intended to climb it. Ihor Zalubniak, whom I had come to respect for his tremendous strength and grit, shook his head. "I wouldn't go there," he said. "It's too hard, and the weather is too severe." I was taken by surprise. Here was a man who seemed to have no qualms about climbing

Mount Logan declaring that Mount Fairweather was too great a challenge. I remembered his remark as we packed, and it added to my anxiety.

Dan and Tom were ready first, so they took off in the little Cessna piloted by Kurt of Gulf Air Taxi at 6:00 pm, and established our first camp on the Grand Plateau Glacier at 2740 metres (9000 ft.). I followed at 8:00 pm on a dramatic and definitely scary flight south. As Kurt turned east toward the landing site on the Grand Plateau Glacier, we flew through heavy clouds and snow. The little plane lurched up and down as lightning lit up the evening sky. Visibility was so bad that I didn't even see the surface of the glacier until we touched down! Dan and Tom had already constructed a bombproof camp, and I stepped onto the glacier relieved and excited.

The spectacular north face of Mount Fairweather loomed above us through the clouds. Although Mount Fairweather is the highest point in British Columbia, three sides of the mountain are in American territory. The north face, the only one wholly in Canada, is guarded by huge hanging glaciers and seracs and has never been climbed. Not anxious to make an early departure from this life, we didn't give it a thought.

The next morning we packed up and started toward Mount Fairweather at 9:45 am. We travelled under sunny skies for five kilometres (3 mi.) to make camp at about 3290 metres (10,800 ft.), just north of the valley that separates Fairweather from its west peak. Travel time was five hours and crevasses were nowhere in sight. Earlier expeditions had pitched their summit camp here, but it would be a very long day; too long. Instead we decided to establish our summit camp higher in the valley. Even from here we could hear the ominous roar of avalanches thundering down the mountain into the little valley we intended to ascend. Alarmed by the almost constant barrage of avalanches, the first party to climb this route decided to detour up and over the west peak to reach the col at the head of the valley. We, on the other hand, chose to tempt fate and move quickly through the danger zone.

Monday morning dawned with snow and whiteout conditions, so we stayed in camp. But when the weather cleared a little in the afternoon, we packed up and climbed into the valley. Huge hanging glaciers on both the right and the left threatened the hollow between Fairweather and its west peak, and the valley floor was littered with avalanche debris for several hundred metres. We simply chose a path up the middle and moved as quickly as we could. Just as we reached what seemed to be the most dangerous point, several tons of ice broke off the west peak and headed in our direction. Tom said, "Well, here it comes!" In what seemed like slow motion, the avalanche roared down the face and across the valley floor. At first, it looked far too small to reach us, but it just kept coming...and coming! Finally the cloud stopped about 50 metres (164 ft.) above us and we breathed a heavy sigh of relief. A few seconds later we were hit by a blast of wind and dusting of snow, all that was left of the avalanche. Once above the hazard, we slogged through deep powder snow. We had snowshoes rather than skis, and the going was very hard on the steepest sections. Dan especially struggled, as the snowshoes he had borrowed were not constructed for inclines and kept sliding backwards. Finally, we made camp at about 3660 metres (12,000 ft.), and turned in weary from the day's floundering. The climb of 2.5 kilometres (1.5 mi.) from our previous camp had taken about four hours. We were in a good position for our summit bid.

That night Mary Fran's telephone rang aboard the Regent Star at 2:00 am. Hoping to get a look at the mountain, she had asked the ship's captain to phone her when the ship was passing Mount Fairweather. She needn't have bothered. The weather had turned nasty, and as if in defiance of its name, Mount Fairweather could not have been seen even at midday.

Tuesday, June 13, the storm continued, and we stayed in camp through a day of whiteout and heavy snow. We had to go out every few hours to clear off the tent to keep it from collapsing. This "Kingdom of Snow" was beginning to show its teeth. It was also becoming clear to me that I would be contending with more than just the mountain on this climb. Three months before I had been troubled by stomach distress and diarrhea. My doctor suspected giardia, a nasty parasite often picked up by campers who drink untreated water. But the illness didn't respond to treatment and the diarrhea continued. Here on Mount Fairweather my condition was getting worse. Every so often I would stumble out into the storm to drop my pants and splatter the snow. Dan looked at me with growing concern and suspicion. Two years before he had been diagnosed with Crohn's disease, an illness that inflames and sometimes blocks the small intestine. The cause of Crohn's disease is not known, although it does seem to be hereditary, and Dan was beginning to recognize my symptoms as his own.

Wednesday also dawned with heavy snow and whiteout conditions, but the weather broke at midday, so we struck out for the summit at 12:30 pm. The upper part of the valley was routine, and except for having to skirt an occasional crevasse, we snowshoed easily to the headwall. With Tom leading, we switchbacked up through deep snow on the right side of the headwall and reached the col at about 4:30 pm. The view from the col was amazing! A wild array of peaks and glaciers stretched off to the south in a lonely, icy wilderness. Unfortunately the view didn't do anything for my gut, and I struggled with another bout of cramps and diarrhea.

A glance up at the steep west peak made us glad we hadn't chosen the route taken by the first party. We were relieved to stand on firm ice at last, and we gladly cached our snowshoes and switched to crampons. The long west ridge stretched above us in the clouds. The angle of the ridge did not look difficult, but it was laced with crevasses. It was a curious sight to see such a prominent ridge adorned with so many crevasses, apparently owing to the enormous snowfall on the mountain. Looking past the mountains, clouds were starting to sweep in from the ocean, and I began to worry about the weather.

After making our way into a small saddle, we started up the first step on the ridge toward a major crevasse. We crossed it on a delicate snow bridge

Dan and Tom Bennett leading up the west ridge.

with only a little difficulty, and continued up the ridge. Tom had been leading all day, so Dan took over for the top part of the ridge and picked up the pace. The ridge was normally hard ice, but occasionally we found ourselves wallowing in deep powder snow. I looked over my shoulder and saw a bank of dark clouds rolling in from the ocean. "Can't we go a little faster?" I shouted up to Dan. He glared back down, "What!" I knew he was pushing the pace hard, but I was beginning to panic with each passing cloud. I remembered that the first ascent party had been battered by a sudden storm only a few hundred metres from the summit. That storm lasted six days.

Finally the slope eased off and we walked onto the broad, flat summit of Mount Fairweather just in time to see a cold sun sink into the Pacific Ocean. It was 10:30 pm on June 14. We hugged each other, then took a few futile pictures in the darkness. Although the view was disappointing in the waning light, we were happy to be on the summit at last.

After a few minutes of celebration, we started down in the dim light of the near-arctic night. As we had left no wands on the ridge, it was a challenge to follow our footsteps. To lose the trail might require us to bivouac for several hours. But each time we seemed to lose it, we regained it again, and eventually found our way back to our snowshoe cache in the col. The rest of the return to camp was routine, and we finally hauled ourselves into our sleeping bags in the faint glow of dawn at 3:30 am. Our summit day from 3660 metres (12,000 ft.) had taken us 10 hours up and five hours down.

The rest of Thursday, June 15, we stayed in camp in unsettled weather.

The weather did not look promising on Friday either, but we packed up and started down at mid-morning. At times it was impossible to distinguish between snow and sky, and we could only feel our way between the wands we left on our ascent. We reached our 3290 metre-high (10,800 ft.) camp for a late lunch, happy to be through avalanche alley for the last time. Then we continued down in fickle weather, hoping to fly out the same day. At times we were in total whiteout, while at other times the clouds broke to reveal a surrounding peak or two. We had a few moments of amusement when we rode the sleds down a steep grade of the Upper Grand Plateau Glacier at breakneck speed: not a mode of glacier travel that I generally recommend!

Finally we reached our first camp at the 2740 metre-high (9000 ft.) landing site on the glacier, and still the weather looked poor. We had just resigned ourselves to at least one more night on the ice when the clouds parted as if by magic. A quick call to Gulf Air and they were on their way.

The author and Tom Bennett on the summit at 11:00 pm.

Gulf Air flew me out to Dry Bay along the coast, then returned to pick up Dan and Tom. I waited in Dry Bay, basking in the sight and smell of spring wildflowers at the take-out point for the Alseck River float trip. Soon we were all back at Yakutat, savouring the showers and good food.

We later learned that our expedition was the only one to Mount Fairweather in 1995. This wild and beautiful mountain clearly deserves more attention. The climb was not technically difficult, except for one or two places on the west ridge where a belay might have been sensible. We were on the climb only five days, far less than I had expected, and we might have stayed longer if it were not for my gut. I felt no better back in Yakutat, and later I was indeed diagnosed with Crohn's disease. For a time I didn't know if I would be able to continue travelling to the remote corners of North America, but fortunately I learned to control my condition with diet and routine, and so far have not required the surgical procedure that Dan needed.

Our confidence was restored. It was time to return to Nirvana.

The Mystery Solved

Wild and wide are my borders,
stern as death is my sway,
And I wait for the men who will win me,
and I will not be won in a day.

A good adventure should have an element of the unknown, and our return to Nirvana in 1996 certainly filled the bill. I was determined not to repeat our mistake of 1993 by trying to go up the Rabbitkettle River. I pored over maps and aerial photographs for hours trying to find a more agreeable approach. At last I spotted a route. It looked like it might be possible to land at a high lake in Hole-in-the-Wall Valley in Nahanni National Park and make our way over the intervening tangle of peaks and high mountain passes. I had no idea how difficult this would be, or even if the east face of Nirvana could be climbed once we reached it. At least two expeditions had seen the east face, but both had decided not to attempt an ascent. The first was led by John Milton in 1961, who described Mount Nirvana (which he called Mount Nahanni) as "rearing its granite head into the gathering storm clouds."[1] Then in 1965, Bill Buckingham came to the east face before circling around to the north for his first ascent. John Milton had landed at Lonely Lake in Hole-in-the-Wall Valley and made his way overland all the way to the foot of Mount Nirvana. He described the second pass he crossed as nearly impassable. But if he could do it, I reasoned, so could we.

Lonely Lake looked like a good landing site. It was only 20 kilometres (12.5 mi.) from Mount Nirvana. But a quick call to the Nahanni Park office was not encouraging. Air landings were not allowed at either Lonely Lake or Hole-in-the-Wall Lake.

"Why not?" I asked.

"We want to prevent overuse of the area," was the reply.

"How often do people go in there?"

"At least one party goes in there almost every year."

One party per year! We certainly didn't want to add to that kind of overuse. It was clear that the park simply didn't want to deal with additional visitors. Still, I decided to write a letter to formalize my request. I signed up Peter Anderson, a geography professor at the University of Montana, and made a case for a scientific expedition. We would make geographic and geological observations along the way, and prepare a report of our findings to Parks Canada. No matter. My request was denied. Parks Canada suggested that we land at a small unnamed lake just outside the park boundary. But this landing site pushed us back 36 kilometres (22.5 mi.) from Mount Nirvana. "By the way," they added, "you'll still have to pay us $75 per person, as you will need to cross through the southwest corner of the park." They wouldn't let us land in the park, but didn't mind extracting $300 from our little party of four for a single night in Nahanni Park.

When I contacted Rob Borelli of Deh Cho Air about our landing, he was equally annoyed. Landing at the little lake suggested by Parks Canada could be unsafe. They would apparently rather we attempt an unsafe landing outside the park than a safe landing inside it. But all considered, I still preferred this alternative to the mosquito bogs of the Rabbitkettle River.

Peter Anderson backed out when he learned of the problem, but we still had a party of four. Dan, who was on an Americorps assignment at Biscayne National Park in Florida, said he could leave early for an expedition in July. Tom was getting married in June, but his fiancée, Hope Malenke, was an avid rock climber and white-water guide who was more than willing to join the climb. They planned to drive to Montana for a warm-up climb on Granite Peak, the highpoint of Montana, then drive north to meet us in the Northwest Territories. Dan and I planned to fly to Edmonton, then drive a rental car 1300 kilometres (812 mi.) up the Alaskan Highway. If all went well, the four Bennetts would meet in Fort Liard, July 13, for our flight to Mount Nirvana.

Dan and I arrived in Fort Liard a little later than we had planned, but still two hours before our scheduled flight time, and strolled into the office of Deh Cho Air. Rob Borelli was waiting for us.

"Hi Rob," I said. "Where are Tom and Hope?"

"Haven't seen them."

I panicked. Would Nirvana continue to curse me with bad luck? Tom and Hope were supposed to have been in Fort Liard hours before. I quickly phoned Ohio, but no one had heard from them there. Finally, only one hour before our scheduled departure, they arrived. I guess you just can't rush honeymooners. We hurried to pack up and get down to the river dock where the DeHaviland Otter waited. But this time I was not so rushed as to forget the food.

We took off on time and began the long flight to Nirvana. The weather looked unsettled and I silently worried that the mountains would be socked in again. If so, we would not be able to make our planned airdrop. If the weather was bad enough, perhaps we could not even land near Hole-in-the-Wall Valley and would have to land at Rabbitkettle Lake after all. The thought of repeating our ordeal of three years ago made me shudder!

As we approached the Ragged Range, the weather lifted a little and our pilot, with the unlikely name of Samo Cebul, manoeuvred skillfully through the granite towers. We were all glued to the windows as the massive peaks and walls flew by. From the air they seemed even more formidable than they had from the ground. I noted that the second pass we had to cross looked evil, perhaps impassable. Finally we approached Nirvana itself, but the mountain was again shrouded in clouds and we were denied even a glance at its still mysterious east face. I quickly turned my attention to a site for the airdrop. The valley immediately east of Mount Nirvana was too rocky and cloistered. I pointed to a relatively smooth glacier southeast of Nirvana where the snow would cushion the shock of impact, and Samo nodded his head. He made a slow pass over the glacier as Tom opened the rear door, pushed out the food bag, and then a bag of climbing gear. We were not flying as low as it had appeared. The bags seemed to tumble through the air forever, then crashed onto the glacier and bounced violently. We hoped that the impact hadn't done too much damage. We also knew that grizzly bears were common in the high country, and that it wouldn't take long for one to devour our precious food.

Samo circled over the Rabbitkettle River and approached the little lake where we were instructed to land. My heart sank! The terrain for the first 9.5 kilometres (6 mi.), between the landing lake and Lonely Lake, was choked with brush and bogs. It looked as bad as the banks of the Rabbitkettle River. Samo banked and came in low over the little lake, carefully checking the wind. I was worried. I could see dark streaks cutting across the water, caused by a strong crosswind. We went straight over the lake and continued west. I glanced at Samo. What was he doing?

"Too dangerous!" he said. "Bad wind direction."

Next we approached Hole-in-the-Wall Lake, 26 kilometres (16 mi.) from Mount Nirvana. Hole-in-the-Wall Lake was large, at least two kilometres (1.25 mi.) long, and in the lee of a huge mountain named Thunder Dome. But even here I could see streaks on the choppy water from the crosswinds.

"Much too dangerous!" Samo said, and kept heading west. The forbidden Lonely Lake lay dead ahead. It was more sheltered and the surface looked relatively smooth.

Samo eased back on the throttle and drifted down to the surface. He offered no explanation, and I was too overjoyed to ask for one. He had landed us a mere 20 kilometres (12.5 mi.) from Mount Nirvana, and a whole day of miserable backbreaking labour was already behind us. I could only think, "Bless you, Samo!"

Samo drifted ashore halfway down Lonely Lake. I briefly considered asking him to taxi all the way to the upper end of the lake, but as I was so grateful just to be there, I said nothing. We quickly unloaded our gear, pushed Samo off, and watched all contact with the civilized world fade into a tiny speck in the sky, then disappear. It was 5:00 pm, July 13.

We shouldered our packs and headed west toward Mount Nirvana. We were thrilled to feel weight on our backs at last and be in full control of the adventure. Whatever the next few days brought us, triumph or tragedy, success or failure, it was ours to make.

The going was not easy at first. We had landed at 1300 metres (4400 ft.), and I was coming to understand that any terrain below 1500 metres (5000 ft.) was likely to be filled with brush and bogs. It took us three hours to make the first five kilometres (3 mi.).

We made our way uphill, first to a small tarn, and finally to a lovely grassy campsite on Beaver Lake at 1500 metres (5000 ft.) Beaver Lake is aptly named, and we heard the beaver splashing their warning alarms far into the night. I finally drifted off to sleep, cradled by the craggy peaks of the Ragged Range. The pressures and charades of the "civilized" world were a distant memory. This world felt genuine and unpretentious. It was not always easy or kind, but it was honest.

The next morning we broke camp, made our way through the low brush around Beaver Lake, and headed up toward the first pass 640 metres (2100 ft.) above us. Beyond Beaver Lake we found ourselves strolling through glorious alpine meadows filled with wildflowers. We couldn't help breaking into an old hiking song:

I love to go a-wandering
along the mountain track,
And as I go I love to sing,
my knapsack on my back.
Oh, may I go a-wandering
until the day I die,
And may I always laugh and sing
beneath God's clear blue sky.

As we neared the first pass, we crossed a snowfield, then scrambled up steep rocks. The view from the pass at 2160 metres (7100 ft.) was amazing. The sheer faces of Nightwind Peak and Promontory Peak, dead ahead, would be our first real challenge. To our left, three dramatic unclimbed towers, identified only as Peaks 18, 19 and 20 on Buckingham's map thrust their granite summits skyward. The route down from the pass was steep but not difficult. Continuing down the valley toward Nightwind Creek, we surprised two mountain goats. They stared at us briefly before climbing powerfully up the mountainside. It occurred to me that they might never have seen two-legged, polypropylene-clad creatures before.

We made camp in a pleasant meadow just above the confluence of Nightwind Creek. So far, so good. After supper we climbed up the hillside to get a better look at the second pass we had to cross. It looked ominous. From our vantage point we could see no obvious break in the ramparts above the Nightwind Lakes toward the west. The next day it rained and we spent a soggy day in camp.

We broke camp the morning of July 16, crossed Nightwind Creek, and headed up toward the barrier above us. We turned left, climbing 240 metres (800 ft.) through lovely meadows to South Nightwind Lake, then spotted a steep couloir leading upward toward the west. Would this couloir lead us to Nirvana? No one knew, but up we went. After climbing another 400 metres (1300 ft.), I was first to reach the crest. We were screwed! Two chutes plunged steeply from the crest, and I could see that neither one led where we wanted to go. One chute curved left back toward South Nightwind Lake, while the other led over a small point and down to North Nightwind Lake (sometimes called Dawnwind Lake). The only route to the west was 150 vertical metres (500 ft.) up sheer cliffs. Tom came up beside me. "I think I could climb it without a pack," Tom said. But with 23-kilogram (50 lbs.) packs on our backs, and with all our climbing gear in the airdrop, it would be an impossible and dangerous struggle. With much regret we turned our backs on the cliffs above and headed back down.

Traversing around toward North Nightwind Lake, we looked at the next pass to the north. It looked steep, and the map showed the other side to be several hundred kilometres straight down.

"That looks much too hard," Dan said. "And all of our climbing gear is in the airdrop on the other side of the mountain. I think we should head for the next pass toward the north. It looks much easier on the map."

"But Dan," I countered, "that will add at least seven kilometres (4.5 mi.) and another whole day to our approach." We were already running behind schedule, and losing another day could be critical. "Besides," I added, "that route takes us all the way down to 1200 metres (3900 ft.); back to the brush and the mosquitoes."

But Dan was firm. "We're exhausted! We simply can't afford to climb another false pass only to come down again." Tom and Hope agreed. So we headed for the pass north of North Nightwind Lake. This was apparently the way that John Milton had come in 1961.

First we had to traverse an enormous boulder field. Boulder fields would come to be the bane of our journey. These awful mazes were filled with boulders the size of cars, and sometimes small houses. Finding a way through was always slow, tiring work. At least the pass, now rising in full view above us, didn't look too difficult from this side.

The climb up the pass was hard, and we were all straining near the top. With full packs, we had already climbed 1100 vertical metres (3600 ft.) that day. So I was surprised when Hope surged ahead in the last few hundred metres. Her energy amazed me. It was here where Hope first earned the nickname "Energizer Bunny," as she just kept going and going, scampering to the pass and taking pictures of us as we struggled to the top. As the days went by I would come to admire her resolve even more. Hope is legally deaf, but has approached life with a determination that won't quit. Despite her handicap, she has earned a college degree in Christian Education, become an expert white-water kayaker and guide, and a competent rock climber. She reads lips with such ease and accuracy that few people would notice she has a disability. Although her life was shattered in 1993 when her father was killed in an airplane crash, she approaches life with a delight and enthusiasm that lift the spirits.

As I crested the pass and looked past Hope's impish face I saw a glacier; a really big one with huge yawning crevasses. The way down didn't look difficult, but we decided to rope up for safety. Hope was thrilled, since this was to be her first glacier travel experience. It was a welcome break for the rest of us too. Though we had counted on a quick glissade down the snow, our plan was frustrated somewhat by several centimetres of heavy granular snow on top of the ice.

Once off the glacier we realized how tired we were. We crossed yet another boulder field, and dragged ourselves down to the shore of a gloomy little lake. It was a poor campsite, but we could go no farther. It was 10:30 pm and we had just had a hard 13 hour-long day. We settled down for supper and a brief rest. It was a dark, dreary little valley that received only brief sunlight, and we named the lake "Dismal Lake." As if to honour its new name, the lake's surface froze overnight.

The next morning, July 17, we broke camp and headed down the valley across seemingly endless boulder fields. At the exit from the valley I looked down at the creek that drains the east side of Nirvana. My heart sank. We would have to go all the way down into the brush, bogs and mosquitoes of the creek, then fight our way up that morass for five long kilometres (3 mi.). I was suddenly depressed.

When we reached the bottom of the valley, it was as bad as I had remembered. Heading up the valley, Dan and I became separated from Tom and Hope in the dense brush. Later, after two hours of struggling up the valley, Dan and I dragged ourselves onto a gravel bar for a rest. I was exhausted, and felt a sudden wave of guilt. Poor Hope! How could I have gotten her into this? She must be several kilometres behind and totally fatigued. Then, not two minutes after we arrived, Tom and the "Energizer Bunny" came bouncing out of the brush, in good spirits and, from all appearances, going stronger than I. It was at that moment that I stopped worrying about Hope.

Farther up the creek it rained so suddenly that we were all soaked, but at last we reached the junction of the streams directly east of Mount Nirvana. The mysterious east face was almost in sight. Only one more stream to cross. But that stream proved unfriendly to Dan, who slipped and fell headfirst into the water. Finally we dragged ourselves up, wet and weary, onto an old glacial moraine and made camp for the night. Since we were just at tree line, we gathered wood and had a glorious fire. Soon everything seemed cheerful and dry again in the glow of the flickering campfire. We had struggled about eight hard-fought kilometres (5 mi.) in as many hours. Tomorrow we would finally be camped at the foot of Mount Nirvana.

The next morning Dan and Tom got up at 7:00 am and left to retrieve the airdrop about 730 metres (2400 ft.) up on the glacier to the south. I was glad they were both feeling strong, as I needed a rest. Later that morning Hope and I kept a vigil and took turns staring up toward the glacier. This was a critical moment. If the airdrop was lost in a crevasse or pillaged by animals, we would not have the equipment to mount a summit attempt and would be half-starved by the time Deh Cho Air picked us up. Straining my eyes, I would focus on a couple of faint specks and imagine them moving, only to decide they were rocks, then move on to the next two specks.

"There they are! I see them. They're coming down!"

I was so relieved that I went up to meet them. The food and the equipment in the airdrop were all okay. We were two or three days behind schedule, but all was again going well.

After lunch we shouldered heavy packs, now 20-30 kilograms (50-60 lbs.) each, and headed toward Nirvana. We climbed 300 metres (1000 ft.) to the meadows east of Nirvana in only an hour and a half, and finally the mountain loomed above us, threatening yet exciting.

The east face of Mount Nirvana resembled a giant reclining pyramid sitting atop a massive concave wall of granite. To its right the sheer walls of the Minotaur, climbed only once from the other side, towered 900 vertical metres (3000 ft.) above the valley floor. Improbable towers and spires rose on every side. We at once began planning our route up the face. Would it go? It looked possible, but I was not confident. The climb would surely be at the very limit of our ability. We began sorting gear and supplies for the climb.

We crawled out of our sleeping bags at 4:15 am, July 19, and were on our way toward the glacier at 5:30 am. The face looked menacing in the dim morning light. But this was what I had come for: the chance to prove to myself that I could still be master of my own destiny. We chose the right side of the Nirvana Glacier.

When we reached the ice we put on crampons and roped up. I led the way through the crevasses. There were no dangers here. The snow had mostly melted, and there were no hidden crevasses lying in ambush beneath thin snow bridges. When we reached the bergschrund, the crack between the glacier and the mountain, it too proved to be no problem. The 'schrund was much smaller than the one on the north side, and we easily passed over a snow bridge to the rock at the bottom of the face.

From here, three rope lengths over loose and broken rock brought us to the bottom of a large steep snowfield in the centre of the face. I led up the snowfield, kicking steps for those behind. When I ran out of rope, Dan stopped belaying and simply started climbing up behind me. Not exactly the best procedure, but eventually we were all standing atop the snowfield. After three more rope lengths over snow and rock, we found ourselves at the bottom of a 150 metre-high (500-ft) band of rock in the centre of the face. We knew that this would be the crux of the route. I felt that if we could climb the next 150 metres (500 ft.), the summit would be ours.

Tom was the best rock climber among us, and this was his moment. It was his task to lead. As leader, he would have no protection above him, and a fall would have serious consequences. The rest of us had the comfort of a top-rope to catch us if we fell. Tom's first lead was up a short friction pitch, aiming for the left end of a large, snow-covered ledge at the top of the rock band. When Tom reached a good spot to belay, Hope and I climbed together behind him. This wasn't exactly by the book. If either Hope or I fell, Tom would have to hold us both on the rope. When Hope and I were up, Dan came up while Tom led the next pitch. This somewhat unorthodox method allowed only one person to lead, while keeping two people climbing at all times. We could climb faster this way, and speed was imperative.

Tom Bennett leading on the 150' rock band on the east fac

On the third lead up the rock band, Tom said, "Oh-oh. This looks interesting!"

I didn't want to hear that. "Interesting" for Tom means "trouble" for me.

"We'll have to cross this wall to reach that crack on the right. It's pretty smooth. Not much to hang on to, and it's wet."

We watched nervously as Tom cautiously worked his way across the wall. It looked hard. But we all managed to struggle across the wet wall, which became the crux move of the route. Tom made a total of six leads up the rock band to bring us at last to the snow-covered ledge. What lay ahead looked anything but easy.

Above us was a steep, evil-looking chimney filled with snow and downsloping ledges. I did not like the looks of it. Still, we felt we must be near the top of the face, so Tom gathered the leader gear and started up. We all watched anxiously. Tom was struggling, and very nearly fell once, then twice. But he wouldn't give up.

"Wait! I think I can make this move," he said.

I had a sudden flashback. Three years before we had been high on the other side of this same mountain, and the climb ended when Tom couldn't make the last few metres. Tom was struggling with the bitterness of that memory too. He nearly fell again.

"Tom, come down," I said.

"Wait. I think I can do it!"

"Maybe so, but I can't. Tom, COME DOWN NOW!" I shouted.

As Tom was making his way back down the chimney, I led straight out across the snowy ledge to the right. Maybe there was another way. After 50 metres (150 ft.) I was literally at the end of my rope. And then I saw it; a narrow little chimney and series of ledges leading left toward the south ridge. It looked like it would go. I shouted for everyone to come over.

When Tom arrived, I took the leader gear and headed up. I ran out the rope and brought Dan up, with Tom and Hope following behind. Dan went straight past me and took the next lead, heading for a large detached flake near the ridge crest. Then I went up past Dan for what looked like the last lead. A final strenuous pull-up in a messy chock-filled chimney, and I was on top of the south ridge. The ridge crest stretched away to the north toward the summit, narrow and exposed, but not difficult. The summit was ours! A flood of relief overcame me.

The detached flake on the final pitch leading to the south ridge.

"It's easy from here," I shouted. "We made it!"

Dan arrived next and led across the ridge crest toward the summit as Tom and Hope came up. I soon became aware that Dan was moving very, very slowly. He had reached a thin arête of snow, not difficult, but terrifically exposed, with nearly 900 metres (3000 ft.) down each side. He was moving cautiously and kicking deep steps, fearing that at any moment the snow might collapse from his own weight.

At the top of the south ridge Dan stepped onto the snowy summit, and I walked up to join him. It was 9:00 pm, July 19. There was the summit cairn, built by Bill Buckingham and Lew Surdam in 1965. The spectacular walls of the Minotaur, now below us, glowed rose-colored in the setting sun. The jagged summits of the Cirque of the Unclimbables pierced the horizon to the north. And just down the north ridge was the place where we had suffered our most bitter defeat three years before. I felt as though I had been preparing for this

Tom, Hope, Jack and Dan Bennett on the summit.

moment all my life. I felt a huge release and wept. This was not the first time that I had cried on a summit, but this time I couldn't stop. It would have been an odd sight to anyone outside our group. Dan held me, his own father, like a baby while I cried.

At last Tom walked onto the summit and we embraced. As Hope came up last we broke into a rousing chorus of "Happy Birthday," for July 19 was the "Energizer Bunny's" birthday. The first woman to climb Mount Nirvana was now 23 years old. A rainbow appeared briefly in the valley, as it did for Bill Buckingham 31 years before, as if to accentuate the beauty of this supremely wild and inviolate place.

We were on the summit about one hour, having a belated lunch and taking the usual summit hero photographs. Then we began the long climb down the east face. It was a slow process. We set up each rappel, then descended the ropes one at a time. After we were all down, we pulled on the ropes and set up the next rappel. Only once did the ropes refuse to come down when a knot jammed in a crack. Fortunately, Tom still had the strength to ascend the ropes and free them. Down we went: across the bergschrund, down the glacier, through the meadows, finally arriving at camp at 9:30 am the next morning. It had been 28 hours since we had crawled out of our sleeping bags. We crashed, and spent the rest of the day sleeping and eating.

We woke up the next morning hoping to do a first ascent in this magnificent range. Dan and Tom left early to climb the massive mountain north of our camp. This summit, known only as Peak #35 on Buckingham's map of 1965, is at an elevation of about 2550 metres (8350 ft.). I was still feeling tired, and so climbed the smaller peak rising above our camp to the south. After reaching the summit and adding a few rocks to the cairn already there, I returned to camp. Dan and Tom climbed the 900 metres (3000 ft.) to the summit of Peak #35 and returned to camp in less than five hours. I watched them return anxiously.

"Well, the good news is we made the summit," Tom said.

"The bad news is that the mountain goats up there have already built a summit cairn," added Dan.

Rats! No first ascent this time.

After a quick lunch we packed up and turned our backs on Mount Nirvana, descending to the stream junction, then climbing up the valley toward the east. We camped in a pleasant little meadow above a lake with ice still on it at about 1700 metres (5600 ft.). I went to sleep nervous about the next day. We had decided to cross the difficult pass where we had failed during our approach. We knew it would be very risky, but we had no desire to retrace our route past Dismal Lake with all the bogs, brush and boulders it had to offer.

The next morning we broke camp and climbed 490 metres (1600 ft.) up Nightwind Peak. The climb was not easy, and the glacier was steep enough to make me wish we had roped up. Arresting a fall would not be easy with 23 kilograms (50 lbs.) on my back. But finally we reached the top of the peak and looked down at South Nightwind Lake. There, 150 vertical metres (500 ft.) below us, was the place where we had turned around six days before, during our approach. But fortunately, rappelling down a sheer face is much easier than ascending it. I had only one concern. I had never tried to rappel with 23 kilograms on my back. I had been told that this much weight has a tendency to turn one upside down, which, naturally, complicates the rappel.

As usual, Tom set up the rappel and was first down the rope. The rest of us followed, and three long, spectacular rappels brought us to the top of the couloir above South Nightwind Lake. Thankfully, no one turned upside down.

Tom and Dan Bennett planning the rappel down the sheer east face of Nightwind Peak.

We descended the couloir, traversed another boulder field, and hiked the meadows back to the site of our second camp. We pulled into camp very tired at 9:30 pm. It had taken us over 10 hours to make 7.5 tough kilometres (4.5 mi.). It rained on and off all the next day, July 23, and we spent the day resting and reading.

We broke camp July 24 at 10:30 am and headed over the last pass toward Lonely Lake. From the pass, Dan and I couldn't miss one last chance to make a first ascent, and we climbed Peak #8 on Buckingham's map. But alas, the precocious mountain goats of the region had constructed another cairn on the summit. Nevertheless, we were treated to a spectacular view of the surrounding mountains, including Mount Nirvana rising majestically to the west. We made camp on the shore of the small tarn between Beaver and Lonely lakes after another tiring 10 hour-long day.

We broke camp one last time in the morning and made our way through the brush down to Lonely Lake. Samo flew in with the Otter at 1:30 pm, spotted us on Lonely Lake, and drifted down to its mirror-like surface. Another few minutes and we were on our magic carpet ride back to civilization.

A few more hours and we were enjoying hot showers, a sumptuous celebration dinner, and clean beds at the Fort Nelson Hotel.

Mount Nirvana is certainly the key to the Canadian highpoints. The long, arduous approach and the complete lack of non-technical routes combine to make this the most formidable highpoint of all. Taking a helicopter directly to the foot of the mountain would certainly diminish the difficulty, but I have the conviction that anyone who does this has not truly climbed the mountain. The moment when I stepped onto the summit of Mount Nirvana was as sweet as any I have ever known. I had lived that moment a hundred times in my dreams, and it did not disappoint me.

Tom and I had six highpoints down and six to go.

[1] "Southern Logan Mountains Expedition," John Miller, Canadian Alpine Journal, 1962, p. 36-38.

Land of the Caribou

There are hardships that nobody reckons;
There are valleys unpeopled and still;
There's a land—oh, it beckons and beckons,
And I want to go back—and I will.
It's the great big broad land 'way up yonder,
It's the forests where silence has lease,
It's the beauty that fills me with wonder,
It's the stillness that fills me with peace.

Nothing is easy, or so it seemed as I hung up the phone. I had just finished a conversation with Johnny May's Air Charter and I was exasperated. Three months before Johnny May had told me that in August he would fly us from Kuujjuaq, Québec to Tallek Arm in the Torngat Mountains and back again. But now the operations manager refused.

"The weather in the Torngats is too unpredictable," he said. "Sometimes we take off from Kuujjuaq, then we have to turn back because of high winds. Sometimes we can't pick up people in the Torngats for days."

"But you *told* me—" I countered. "I bought airline tickets to Kuujjuaq!"

"Sorry. We're too busy with hunters in August. If we have one day of bad weather, we have no place to move on our schedule. No can do."

Now I understood. Hunters stream into northern Québec in August. Catering to hunters was their cash cow, and they couldn't afford to jeopardize that business for a few climbers.

Johnny May's sudden refusal to fly us into the mountains left me scrambling for another alternative. I phoned Atsanik Lodge at Nain on the coast of Labrador. They run weekly boat trips to the Torngat Mountains for $800 per person. I had at first rejected this option because both Tom and I tend to get seasick. I could easily picture the two of us a sickly green, hanging over the rail for two days up and two days back: not a pretty sight. I need not have worried, however, as the boat trips to the Torngats had all been filled long before.

Next, I phoned Air Inuit, the only other charter service to fly out of Kuujjuaq. I wasn't hopeful. I already knew that Air Inuit only flew wheeled aircraft, and there was no landing strip in the Torngat Mountains.

But to my surprise, Air Inuit said, "Sure, no problem. We can land you on a gravel bar only 14 kilometres (9 mi.) south of Mont d'Iberville. The weather is great in the Torngats in August."

The only problem was cost. Air Inuit flies twin engine DeHaviland Otters out of Kuujjuaq, and the cost for both drop-off and pick-up in the Torngat Mountains was $7,053. Ouch! We had only four people going on this trip, and it was too big a price tag to split four ways. I needed to think of another plan.

It was then that I noticed that the Air Inuit landing site was on the bank of the Koroc River, a river that flowed west toward Kangiqsualujjuaq (say that fast three times!), another small Inuit village in northern Québec. Why not put two canoes in the Otter, then after climbing the mountain canoe down the river and get picked up by Johnny May in a smaller and cheaper float plane? Johnny May's Air Charter reluctantly agreed, but Air Inuit decided that it could stuff only one canoe in the Otter. Nothing seemed to be working out.

Then Tom had an idea. He suggested we take two shredders, neoprene white-water boats that deflate into a suitcase-size package of about 16 kilograms (35 lbs.) each. We could simply inflate the shredders, travel 140 kilometres (87 mi.) downriver, then deflate the boats for the short flight back to Kuujjuaq. I was beginning to like the sound of this. Not only would we save money, but we would also have the adventure of floating down a remote whitewater river that descended 260 metres (850 ft.) over the total distance of 140 kilometres (87 mi.). I had no idea of the difficulty of the water, but Tom and Hope were both expert white-water river guides. The plan seemed perfect. Finally, Tony Daffern, the fourth member of our expedition, found someone who had been down the Koroc and was able to describe the rapids in detail.

After the plans were made and each detail attended to, I dashed off with Mary Fran and Jennifer to do the highpoints of the three Maritime provinces. Tom couldn't get the extra time off to do the Maritimes and Ontario, and it was now becoming apparent that he would not be able to finish the project with me that year. I returned from the Maritime provinces August 8, 1997, and had only three days to prepare for our trip to northern Québec.

Tom and Hope drove up from Georgia August 10, and the next day we caught a late flight to Montréal where we planned to overnight before the long flight to Kuujjuaq.

I finally met Tony Daffern, the fourth member of our expedition, at the Ramada Inn near Montréal's Dorval Airport. Tony was the publisher of Rocky Mountain Books, where I had submitted a proposal for this book. Tony had taken an interest in my Canadian highpoint project, decided to publish my book and to join us on our expedition to the highpoints of Québec and Newfoundland. Tony was instantly likable, with an infectious smile and an obvious British accent. He was, like me, an aging warrior with thinning hair, and I identified with him at once. Tony was an experienced hiker and climber, but had no white-water experience and was a little nervous about that portion of the journey. I briefly wondered whether my Rocky Mountain Books contract would be cancelled if the publisher drowned during the trip. Tony assured me that it would.

The next morning we hauled our gear back to the airport for our First Air flight north. While waiting in the check-in line, Hope noticed a small brown animal in a crate beside us.

"Oh, what a cute dog!" Hope said off-handedly.

"That's not a dog. It's a chicken," the owner curtly replied.

Hope was taken aback. "A chicken?"

"Yes. She's Zelda; Zelda the psychic chicken."

Hope paused again, "A psychic chicken?"

"Yes. Zelda is going to Kuujjuaq to perform her act. She's never flown before and she's a little nervous about the flight."

As Zelda the psychic chicken was worried about the flight, I wondered if I should be worried too. But it went well and we landed on schedule in Kuujjuaq at 11:30 am.

Our early arrival in Kuujjuaq allowed us to schedule our flight to the Torngats the same day, and by 2:30 pm we were winging our way east toward the Torngat Mountains. The land below was spectacular, with unnamed rivers tumbling down through desolate canyons toward the sea. The hills were barren, but with countless caribou trails worn into the tundra, visible even from a few thousand metres up. As we approached the mountains the weather became unsettled. Finally the Selamuit Range came into view and we could just make out the ragged Koroc Ridge of Mont d'Iberville through the darkening clouds. The sight was encouraging. The mountains were not particularly steep, and only the final several metres of the ridge looked difficult. It was definitely doable.

Our Air Inuit pilot circled for a landing, though I failed to see anything below that could be called a landing strip. He made a final approach toward a small, rough gravel bar 200 metres (656 ft.) south of the Koroc River. It looked like a postage stamp. I glanced wide-eyed back at Tom, Hope and Tony, and we held our collective breath as the Otter bumped down and rolled to a stop with little room to spare. What seemed like a life-threatening experience to us was obviously a routine landing for Air Inuit.

It was great to finally be on the ground in this beautiful, stark land. As always, I was anxious on the flight in. But now we were in our element and back in control. We happily unloaded our gear and supplies, and watched Air Inuit disappear into the western sky. It was the last of civilization we would see for the next nine days.

Our first problem was to haul our gear to the river and pump up the shredders. Tom instructed us as we took turns with the hand pump. The shredders had to be pumped up to just the right degree. Too little air and they would be floppy and unmanageable; too much air and they might rupture, especially in hot sun. A damaged shredder would be a serious dilemma, as one shredder could not possibly carry all four of us plus gear and supplies.

Hope Bennett sitting on a "shredder" taking a picture of caribou along the Koroc River.

Tony and I tied our gear onto the first shredder, jumped aboard and pushed off into the shallow Koroc River. We needed to travel five kilometres (3 mi.) downriver to reach our first campsite, the place where we would head north toward Mont d'Iberville. The river here was split into many channels and filled with sandbars. We had to get out frequently and drag the shredder over sand to reach the next channel. The weather was gloomy, and the water bitterly cold. This was hard work, and not exactly what I had had in mind. But the river finally improved and we floated quietly down past grazing caribou, arriving at our planned campsite at 6:30 pm. Just a few hours before we had checked out of the Ramada Inn in Montréal, and yet here we were, deep in the mysterious Selamuit Range of the Torngat Mountains. We drifted off to sleep content, dreaming of the climb ahead.

The next morning I stuck my head out of the tent into a brilliant cloudless day, the sun gleaming off the water. A female caribou and her calf cautiously approached our tents, curious to see what had arrived. We had made camp among some high sandbars along the river, a good place to leave the shredders for a few days. The caribou disappeared behind a sandbar for a few minutes, only to reappear above our tents for a closer look. The caribou that wandered around our camp that morning were permanent residents, but every spring and summer these mountains are witness to one of the greatest spectacles on earth. The largest caribou herd in the world, the George River herd, numbering 700,000 animals, migrates through the southern Torngats. I could hardly imagine such a sight.

The caribou had distracted me from my breakfast preparation. I walked over to a nearby stream for water and noticed several large animal tracks. "Wow, must be a small bear," I thought. I had noticed the tracks the night before, but never guessed their true origin. Then we saw them. Two large gray wolves watched us from the riverbank. They were wary, and didn't approach as closely as the caribou, but their curiosity and concern were obvious. At last the wolves retreated back down the river and began howling mournfully. "We are here," they howled, "and this is our territory!" Surely there is nothing as magical and thrilling as the howling of wolves in the wild.

After a quick breakfast, we began packing for the climb. Seeing the wolves had given us a new concern. We had to leave the shredders and a large cache of food behind for at least three days while we climbed Mont d'Iberville. Would the wolves dig up our cache, leaving us without food for the rest of the trip? Even worse, would they chew on the neoprene shredders in our absence? We didn't know, but we had no choice other than to hope that their instincts would keep them away. We deflated the shredders and buried our supplies under a few rocks. We then started up the long, broad valley toward Mont d'Iberville to the constant howling of the wolves. "This is our land," they wailed. "You don't belong here!"

Hiking up the valley was even easier than I had hoped. There were no brush or trees to bushwhack, and no awkward boulder fields to negotiate. We simply walked through grassy open meadows under sunny skies. Occasionally a curious caribou would approach to look us over. It occurred to me that the wolves must have an easy time dining on caribou up here. It took only 4.5 hours to walk the 10 kilometres (6 mi.) up the valley, and we made camp by a small unnamed lake beneath the Koroc Ridge in the early afternoon. Our camp was at 560 metres (1850 ft.), only about 1100 metres (3600 ft.) below the summit of d'Iberville.

The next day, August 14, we were up at 5:15 am, and after a quick breakfast were on our way up the Koroc Ridge at 6:10 am. We climbed a steep, snow-filled gully directly above our camp. At the top of the couloir we turned right, up rocky slabs toward the crest of the main Koroc Ridge. I was beginning to worry about the weather. Low clouds had formed, and were moving fast across the tops of the peaks. Tony set a good pace and reached the ridgecrest first. When I arrived, the summit of Mont d'Iberville was partially obscured by clouds, and the knife-edge ridge leading to the summit looked more formidable than it had from the air. After a brief rest we pushed on to where the Koroc Ridge was joined by the west ridge, and we stood for the first time on the boundary between Québec and Newfoundland. After climbing farther toward d'Iberville, we came upon two cairns. We were apparently not the first climbers to come this way.

Beyond the cairns the ridge became spectacular, narrow and exposed, dropping hundreds of metres down either side. At times it took courage to walk upright on the narrow ridge with a strong wind gusting in from the west. I was still not sure the weather would let us reach our goal, which

Hope and Tom Bennett, and Tony Daffern on the summit of Mount Caubvick, highest point in Newfoundland. The picture was taken from the summit of Mont d'Iberville.

sometimes disappeared from view into the turbulent clouds. We skirted a few pinnacles until we reached the final drop leading down to an orange-red notch. Here, sometime in the distant past, a wall of molten lava had erupted up into the bedrock, forming a dike. The heat from the lava turned the rocks red, and the softer volcanic rocks eroded away faster than the surrounding granite, making a notch. This was too precarious to climb unroped, so we set up an anchor and rappelled into the notch. As Tom and Hope finished their rappel, Tony and I reconnoitred the route ahead. The first orange pinnacle in the notch we traversed on the right. In the second pinnacle, we found a narrow slot on the left. By taking off our packs, we could just slip through this "fat-man's misery" to the bottom of the notch. The ridgecrest ahead looked steep, but not too difficult, so we left the rappel rope in place to use on our return. The weather was holding.

After climbing the final ridgecrest, we stepped onto the summit of Mont d'Iberville at 11:10 am. Clouds were blowing on and off the summit, at times revealing a spectacular landscape. Toward the west, the mountain plunged steeply to a narrow watershed leading north to Tallek Arm. A breathtaking drop on the north side fell away to Ice-Blue Tarn, still frozen even in mid-August. Stretching off toward the east was the Minaret Ridge, used by most climbers of this mountain. The Minaret Ridge did not look difficult from our vantage point. Just to the right, a small ridge rose from the valley where we had camped to join the Minaret Ridge. This certainly would have been an easier approach than the one we had taken.

We then turned our attention to Mount Caubvick, the highest mountain in Newfoundland. From the summit of Mont d'Iberville, we walked about 10 metres (33 ft.) along the north ridge into Labrador. Here a small crest rose about one metre (3.3 ft.) higher than anything in Québec. In a cairn constructed at the top of Mount Caubvick we found the register left years before by Cliff Holtz, and dutifully signed our names. I had now climbed 11 Canadian highpoints, with only Ontario to go. After taking a few pictures, we started back down the Koroc Ridge at 11:45 am.

Soon after starting down, the summit was engulfed by clouds. We climbed back through the dike notch and around the pinnacles, reaching the cairns at the top of the ridge for a belated lunch. It was here that the wisdom of bringing Tony along was revealed. The food that I bring on these trips is little more than sustenance. Dinners are mostly dehydrated food, and the lunches are especially uninspired. But I had assigned Tony the job of bringing lunches, and they were glorious: corned beef, sardines, salmon and home-baked fruitbread. We ate better than I do at home!

We returned to lake camp at 4:00 pm. Clouds had continued to build, and we had a cold, gray evening in camp. But the weather couldn't dampen the glow of our success. It was a memorable day, especially climbing the exposed knife-edge ridgecrest south of the dike notch. We turned in content at 8:30 pm.

We arose early the next morning and headed back down the valley to our cache at the river. Luckily, the wolves had not bothered our supplies. As we pumped up the shredders, there was excitement in the air. We were about to start down a steeply descending river far from civilization with little knowledge of the hazards that lay ahead. I felt a little like one of my boyhood heroes, Major John Wesley Powell, who became the first person to descend the Colorado River through the Grand Canyon. "What falls there are, we know not," he said. "What rocks beset the channel, we know not; what walls rise over the river, we know not."[1] Of course, many people had navigated the

The author climbing out of the notch on the descent. Photo Tony Daffern.

Koroc River before, and Tony had even talked with someone who had paddled it in a kayak. Still, there was an air of adventure as we pushed off into the swift current.

The river here was small, and at times disappeared into rock gardens that could not be navigated. Several times we had to get out and drag the shredders over rocks to reach deeper water below. It was hard work, and the cold water quickly numbed our feet. We finally made camp at 5:00 pm on the left bank just below a long stretch of seven "rapids," which were actually tedious rock gardens. Despite the troublesome rocks, we had made 17 kilometres (10.5 mi.) and were pleased at our progress. I felt that the river could only improve as it increased in volume downriver.

The next morning, August 16, we were on the river again at 8:00 am. We passed the divide that led to the Palmer River on the north, and turned south. Then, just as I was convincing myself that the worst was behind us, we came upon a huge monotonous rock garden. There was no way through. We had to drag the shredders over rocks and across gravel bars for more than a kilometre (0.6 mi.). It was backbreaking work. This was not the sort of river trip that I had had in mind.

Late in the afternoon we came across a grim reminder of the hazards of wilderness travel: a canoe and heap of gear had been left along the riverbank. Their owners had just begun a trip down the Koroc when they received word that two of their friends had been killed. They died when their small plane crashed into a mountain. They were Marie-Soleil Tougas and Jean-Claude Lauzon, well-known French-Canadian television personalities. Grief-stricken, their friends had helicoptered out to attend their funerals, leaving their gear behind.

That night I stayed up to watch a golden sunset kiss the barren summit of Mount Haywood, then turned in weary from the day. Late that night, Tony woke me up. "Jack, come out and see!" When I looked out, a shimmering curtain of silver and ghostly green danced across the sky. We watched spellbound as the northern lights swirled in the night sky. I could easily understand why the early Inuit regarded these mysterious lights as the dancing spirits of the dead. It was a fitting climax to our day on the remote and beautiful Koroc River.

The next morning we were on the river again at 8:00 am, and made good time now that the river was bigger. The rapids now came bigger and faster. Here the shredders, which are true white-water boats, showed their full advantage. Shredders are made of tough neoprene, and are seemingly indestructible. They resemble a catamaran in shape, with a large inflated tube on each side, and smaller inflated crossmembers that give the boat its shape. The bottom of the shredder is uninflated, with holes to let the water out—and in. A passenger of a shredder must resign himself to having wet feet. In rapids, the shredder bounces and bucks like a bronco. Tom reminded us to keep at least one foot wedged firmly under the tube to keep from being tossed into the water. But it was all great fun. We ran a big Class V rapid just beyond the Naksarulak River, and sped on toward the "Chutes Korluktok," the falls of the Koroc River.

The author and Tom Bennett ferry a loaded shredder through the rapids. Photo Tony Daffern.

A large black bear was fishing above the falls, and dashed off over the hill as we approached. He was big and powerful, and obviously well fed. The black bear is another unusual resident of this remarkable land. The Torngat Mountains are the only place in North America where black bears, normally forest-dwelling animals, roam free on the open tundra.

The chutes of the Koroc are a dramatic 12 metre-high waterfall, followed by several smaller falls and cataracts. Here we had one of Tony's marvellous lunches, and revelled in the scenery of that magnificent place. After lunch we portaged the chutes on a faint, but reasonably good trail on the left bank, and made camp for the night near the mouth of the "Ruissseau Sukaliuk," the Sukaliuk River, about 30 kilometres (19 mi.) downriver from our last camp.

The next morning we slept late and were not on the river until 9:00 am. It didn't seem to matter, as we were now way ahead of schedule. The river was larger and faster now, and we ran some exciting Class IV rapids just below camp. After lunch the wind changed direction, and for the first time we were battling a stiff headwind. Here the shredders proved to be at a serious disadvantage. Their high profile and lack of a keel made them practically impossible to paddle upwind. Paddling into the wind was tiring, and we made camp just beyond a big island in the river. We had covered 27 kilometres (17 mi.).

As we descended the river, we began to encounter more and more trees and brush along the bank, and with them, swarms of mosquitoes and black flies. The mosquitoes weren't so bad, but the persistent hordes of black flies were becoming unbearable. Even when we were paddling, the black flies crawled up our pantlegs and down our collars, inflicting irritating bites on our legs and necks. The farther down the river we went, the worse they became. The black flies seemed especially voracious when someone had to drop his pants, an act that never failed to send them into a feeding frenzy.

The morning of August 19 we were on the river at 7:30 am in a futile effort to escape the flies. After running the first set of rapids, an ominous roar signalled a menacing rapid ahead. Tony and I looked at the violent drop and decided that a little discretion was in order. We portaged the rapid on the left bank. But for Tom and Hope, this was their element. They were both white-water guides, and would on occasion even paddle their kayaks over 10 metre-high (33 ft.) waterfalls. The rapid featured an enormous hydraulic on the left, where water poured in from all directions. Any boat caught in such a hydraulic would be sucked under immediately. Tom and Hope carefully ferried their shredder to the right side of the river, then paddled ahead into a hole only slightly less fearsome. Together with their shredder, they disappeared briefly, then popped up and careened wildly down the river. Tony and I watched in alarm, but for Tom and Hope it was just another day at the office.

We ran a few more fun rapids with big waves, then the fun was over. From there it was only flat water all the way to the pick-up point. We made camp early that day after only 23 kilometres (14 mi.) on the river owing to a persistent headwind and even more persistent black flies. After a hasty dinner we retreated to the safety of the tents.

The next day, August 20, was our last full day on the Koroc River. The river was big here, broad and meandering around countless sandbars. It seemed impossible to choose the right channel. Inevitably our little passageway would dwindle, forcing us to drag our shredder over the sand to reach another channel. The day was made doubly hard by the headwind, which continued strong throughout the day.

Finally we pulled into the pick-up point; an old deserted hunting camp on the right bank. The camp was littered with junk: old mattresses, heaps of trash, and literally piles of caribou jawbones. I found it hard to imagine that shooting these curious sociable creatures would be much sport. We placed our camp out on a small point in the wind, hoping to confound the flies. It didn't work.

The next day, August 21, was our last day on the river, but I had requested a late pick-up in case we were running late. I now wished Johnny May was coming earlier. Tony's lunches aside, our diet was beginning to wear on me, and I fantasized constantly about plates full of pizza and steak. My mind wandered back to Zelda the psychic chicken. I wondered if she was still in Kuujjuaq, and whether she would look best regular or extra crispy.

Tony and I decided to hike up a mountain above the hunting camp to escape the black flies. It worked, and soon Tom and Hope joined us for a pleasant day high above the Koroc. From the mountain we could see all the way out to Ungava Bay where giant white icebergs glistened in the sun. Later that day we hiked back down in time to catch the Johnny May float plane that buzzed up the river like a giant red mosquito. Our adventure in the Torngat Mountains was at an end. The next day we boarded the 11:00 am flight back to Montréal and civilization.

[1] *Beyond the Hundredth Meridian*, Wallace Stegner, Penguin Books, 1954, p.96.

The Maritime Provinces and Ontario

Here by the camp-fire's flicker,
Deep in my blanket curled,
I long for the peace of the pine-gloom,
When the scroll of the Lord is unfurled,
And the wind and the wave are silent,
And world is singing to world.

Jenny was just ahead of us, bouncing from rock to rock like a little grasshopper, her pink poncho flapping wildly in the wind. At times she was barely visible through the sleet and clouds sweeping across Mount Mansfield. Mary Fran and Jenny were getting their first taste of mean mountain weather, and they didn't like it.

On July 28, 1997, we had loaded up our Jeep Cherokee and headed toward the Maritime provinces of Canada. Mary Fran and Jenny were beginning to collect US highpoints, so we decided to savour a few New England mountains on the way through. We first drove up Mount Greylock, the highpoint of Massachusetts, then drove on to Mount Mansfield, the highest point in Vermont. At the top of the road on Mount Mansfield, a warden advised us against going to the top. The summit was about 2.5 kilometres (1.5 mi.) away, along an exposed rocky ridge, and the weather was unsettled. But highpointers are incurable optimists and not easily dissuaded, so we set out for the summit in threatening weather.

At first all seemed to go well. We reached the summit, took a few pictures and enjoyed the view. Then, just as we were starting down, I looked over my shoulder and saw evil weather bearing down on us. For me, this was a familiar story, but to Mary Fran and Jenny, it was a new and frightening experience. "Better hurry up!" I said, but it was too late. Soon the wind heightened to gale force, and rain and sleet began peppering our faces. At times we could only hunker down and hang on to avoid being blown off our feet. But Jenny just kept bouncing on ahead, and we finally reached the shelter of the Jeep.

Mary Fran had acquired a newfound respect for the kind of weather that mountains can suddenly brew up.

Two days later we took the little cog railway to the top of Mount Washington, the highpoint of New Hampshire, and the highest point in the northeastern United States. Again, the weather turned foul, and we ran from the shelter of the summit restaurant to the highest spot among the rocks, then ran back again. Mount Washington was living up to its reputation as having some of the worst recorded weather in the country. The weather station at the summit has recorded winds up to 370 km (231 mi.) per hour, the highest measured wind velocity on the surface of the earth. We returned to the Jeep and drove on to Canada, hoping for an improvement in the weather.

Nova Scotia

"You'll never make it," Dennis Doyon stated flatly. "The last group to go in there was the Canadian military. They were on a wilderness training exercise, and it took search-and-rescue three days to find them." This was cause for serious concern. As the owner of Sea Spray Cycle Centre, Dennis knew the Cape Breton Highlands well. His advice was not to be taken lightly.

The topographic map from the Canada map office showed a trail leading past Franey Mountain, just north of Ingonish, to within one kilometre (0.6 mi.) of White Hill, the highpoint of Nova Scotia. It was 30 kilometres (19 mi.) long round-trip, but I reasoned it could be done in one day if I went light and fast. The trip could be made easier if I rented a mountain bike from Dennis' Cycle Centre in nearby Smelt Brook, and rode at least part of the way on the bike. But maps can be deceiving. What looked like a trail on the map was actually an old fire road. And the fire roads on the Cape Breton Highlands hadn't been maintained in years, ever since the job of fire patrolling had been done with aircraft.

"That old road is so overgrown with spruce and alders that you probably won't even be able to follow it. Once you lose the road out there, you'll be in big trouble!"

I could tell that Dennis wasn't exaggerating. He was dead serious. But a highpointer doesn't usually listen to reason.

"What could it hurt just to give it a try?" I thought. "If it gets really bad, I'll just turn back."

I was afraid that Dennis, knowing my plans, would refuse to rent me one of his bikes, so I pretended to be interested in some other trip.

"Oh well. What a shame!" I feigned. "What other day-trip could you recommend for me?"

I listened patiently while he described another mountain bike trail. I asked lots of questions about the route, hoping to convince him that I wasn't really going to try the old fire road to White Hill. But I didn't fool Dennis for a minute.

"Good luck!" he said as we drove off. I could tell from the tone of his voice that he knew where I was headed.

It was 5:00 am, August 3, when I roused Mary Fran from her sleep in the MacDonald Motel. With Jenny, I didn't even try. I just carried her out to the Jeep and plopped her asleep on the back seat. We drove 65 kilometres (40 mi.) south to the Franey Mountain road, then up to the last parking area at the national park boundary, about 170 metres (550 ft.) above sea level. Mary Fran looked concerned as I unloaded the mountain bike.

"When should I notify the authorities?" she asked.

"Certainly not before 10:00 pm," I replied. I wasn't sure just how long this was going to take, so I asked her to check back at the Atlantic Restaurant north of Ingonish every half hour beginning at 5:00 pm.

I was off on the bike at 6:20 am. I decided to go as light as possible, carrying only rain gear, lunch and water in a small daypack. The Franey Mountain trail was well used as far as the old fire lookout tower. The road climbed through dense spruce forest, gaining about 200 metres (650 ft.) in the first 2.5 kilometres (1.5 mi.). I was climbing in the bike's lowest gear, and sweating heavily despite the chill of the morning air.

Finally I spotted the old fire road branching off to the right at about 365 metres (1200 ft.) above sea level. It was barely visible through the dense undergrowth. It looked like Dennis was right. I pushed the bike only a few metres into the brush, and decided that it was futile. If I were going to reach White Hill, it would have to be on foot. I hid the bike in the bushes and started walking at 7:00 am.

By looking for a slight passage through the larger spruce trees I was able to follow the old road. At times I had to push through the alders without quite knowing where I was going. After about eight kilometres (5 mi.) on the old road I came into an open boggy meadow and the road disappeared completely. Faint ruts in the bog hinted at the way, but they were nearly impossible to follow. I turned around and looked back, trying to fix the location of the road in my mind for the return trip. I took a compass heading across the meadow as a precaution. If I did get lost it would probably be here, and I would be in serious trouble. Travel was difficult enough on the old fire road, but pushing through the bush would be impossible if I ever lost the trail.

After the meadow the road improved, and I reached the trail junction south of Lake-of-Islands by 10:00 am. By this time I had covered about 12 kilometres (7.5 mi.) on foot. Things were going according to plan for a change. I continued west on the fire road another 2.5 kilometres (1.5 mi.) past the north shore of White Hill Lake, to a point directly north of White Hill. The highpoint, a low brush-covered mound, was only one kilometre (0.6 mi.) away. But here I got a taste of what bushwhacking on the highlands was really like. Thick low growth made footing nearly impossible, and the short dense spruce seemed impenetrable. It was nasty going, but the higher I got, the less dense the brush became. Finally, I could see the highest point.

"Oh my God," I thought. "What's that?"

There ahead of me was what appeared to be a red-and-white hitching rail for horses. Had I hiked all that way, and pushed through all that brush, when

The survey marker atop White Hill, Nova Scotia.

there was a horse trail up here? But as I walked closer I could see it was only an old radio tower, blown down by the wind. And there was the Canadian survey marker atop a short concrete block. The view was not spectacular, but was made special by the effort I had taken to get to it. I breathed a heavy sigh of relief. It was 11:15 am.

I started down after 30 minutes on the summit. My day was still only half over. Unless I managed to stay on the road on the way back, I would be spending a miserable night on the highlands, to say nothing of the consequences of launching an embarrassing and expensive rescue effort. I paused just long enough for lunch at the fire road junction east of White Hill.

At about 2:00 pm I reached the meadow where the road all but disappeared. I strained to follow the old ruts through the meadow, but on the other side, the fire road was nowhere to be seen.

"No need to panic," I thought. "I'll just double back and find where I went wrong." I was struggling to think clearly and maintain my composure.

After about 20 minutes of careful searching, I found it, an obscure breach in the bushes where the old road used to go.

The rest of the hike back to Franey Mountain was routine, though I was weary from the long day. I found the bike where I had left it, and cycled down to the Atlantic Restaurant at 4:45 pm. Mary Fran was relieved to see me so early. We returned the bike to Sea Spray Cycle Centre, and I hobbled into a restaurant for the customary celebration dinner.

White Hill had been a challenging and satisfying highpoint. I had covered 30 kilometres (19 mi.) on foot, plus a few more on the bike, in about 10 hours. The old fire road past Franey Mountain is now very difficult to follow, and will only get worse as the years go by. The slightly longer, but better maintained trail past Lake-of-Islands would probably be a better future choice.

We spent the next day revelling in the unique beauty and living history of Cape Breton Island. We will not soon forget the rugged coastline and quaint fishing villages of this beautiful place. We took time to drive north to Bay Saint Lawrence for a whale-watching cruise, and delighted in watching dozens of pilot whales frolic around our boat.

Prince Edward Island

The exact location of the highpoint of Prince Edward Island is a puzzle. The topographic map shows three separate areas south of Fredericton above the 135-metre (450-ft.) contour line. I decided that if I couldn't find out which was higher, I would go to all three.

We headed south from Fredericton, past a radio tower, then turned left on Highway 227. It looked as though it would be impossible to pick out the highest point among the rolling hills. Just then I spotted a man and his wife working in their garden, and drove up their driveway. The man had the interesting name of Winston Churchill Hurry.

"Oh yes," he nodded knowingly. "The highest point is just up the road in that potato field. I'll take you there."

We drove up the dirt road, parked the Jeep, and walked up a little knoll in the potato field. It was certainly the highest point of the land nearby, but what about the other two areas above 135 metres (450 ft.)?

The author and wife, Mary Fran, in the potato field at the highpoint of Prince Edward Island.

Mary Fran and Jenny Bennett at the fire tower on Mount Carleton, highest point in New Brunswick.

"They used to think the highest point was over there," he said, pointing to the west, "but we now know that it's right here."

Mary Fran seemed amused by this silly "highpoint," but to a highpointer, no real highpoint is frivolous. Mary Fran and I stood on the sacred spot while Winston Churchill Hurry took our picture. Was this really the highest point? It was the largest of the three areas, and that together with Mr. Hurry's conviction was good enough for me. (Note: A recent survey shows the highpoint as a benchmark about 100 metres from the road just inside the wood.)

We piled back into the Jeep and headed for New Brunswick.

New Brunswick

It was August 6, 1997, a very significant day. It was Mary Fran's 50th birthday, and she wanted to do something special. Not that Mount Carleton, the highpoint of New Brunswick, was a colossal challenge or a risky ascent, but it was a statement that she still had things to strive for; mountains to climb.

Once again, I carried a sleeping Jenny to the Jeep in front of our room at the Coastal Inn in Grand Falls, New Brunswick. It took one hour and 40 minutes of driving through the fog and sleepy New Brunswick villages to reach the Mount Carleton trailhead. Jenny was finally awake, and we started up the east trail at 9:20 am.

The trail climbed gently through mature spruce, fir and yellow birch. After about an hour we came upon the old towermen's cabin, a Spartan cottage where the men who used to man the Mount Carleton fire tower sheltered during storms or when off duty. I found myself wondering what their life would have been like. Most of the time they sat in the glassed-in tower perched on top of Mount Carleton, scanning the forest for smoke. For many years there was only one towerman, a truly lonely life. Then, because of safety and isolation, two went on duty. If it was wet weather, they might take turns working on the trails leading to the tower or bringing up supplies. During the nighttime or on rainy days the towermen would be in the cabin with only their books, hobbies and local animals for company.

Past the cabin, the trail climbed more steeply, and we caught a glimpse of the bare, craggy summit of Mount Carleton through the trees. Once above the trees, the trail became steep and rocky, and a lovely panorama of mountains and lakes surrounded us. A little square fire tower sat on the highest point. Here the towermen had sat from May to October of every year between 1923 until 1968, before airplanes were used for patrolling. If a towerman spotted smoke, he would turn the alidade, a brass sighting device, over a map in the centre of the floor. Then using a crank telephone, he would call headquarters with an exact bearing and estimated distance.

The weather was crystalline and the sky a dark blue. We sat on the steps of the fire tower and had lunch in the warm sunshine. This made up for many a stormy summit. The hike to the top had taken only a little over two hours, and after about an hour on top, we walked down in an hour and a half.

We drove back to Great Falls, then to Ohio for a rendezvous with Tom and Hope. I had only a few days to pack before heading to northern Québec to climb Mounts d'Iberville and Caubvick.

Ontario

It was early September 1997, and I was feeling anxious. I had now climbed 11 of the 12 Canadian highpoints. Only Ontario remained. I had at first planned to go to Ontario with Tom and Hope directly after we returned from Québec, but they were impatient to get back to Georgia, and were both feeling a little burned out. Then I thought that Dan might go up with me in September. But Dan had a new girlfriend, and his priorities were elsewhere. I felt I had to complete the project that fall, but how? Who could I get to go with me? Ishpatina Ridge, the highpoint of Ontario, was deep in Lady Evelyn-Smoothwater Provincial Park, and required at least three days of paddling through high wilderness lakes. And several long portages were required. Surely I couldn't carry a canoe plus all my camping gear across the portages by myself.

Then I had an idea. Under my deck was an old fiberglass kayak I had made 25 years before. It weighed only 13 kilograms (28 lbs.). Perhaps if I took the kayak and went super-light, I could go by myself. The more I thought about the idea, the more I liked it. The hike to White Hill in Nova Scotia had been my first long trek alone, and I found it surprisingly enjoyable. The thought of tackling the trip to Ishpatina Ridge by myself, and confronting all the unknowns and hardships alone took on a peculiar appeal. And so I strapped my little kayak to the top of my Saturn coupe on September 25, and headed north. I drove nearly 1200 kilometres (750 mi.) in a miserable rain, and managed to find my way in the dark down a series of small dirt roads south of Gowganda to the Beauty Lake Road bridge across the Montréal River. I spent an uncomfortable, cold night sleeping in the car.

The next morning the river was enveloped in a heavy fog, and a cold sun was straining to break through the mist. It was a beautiful and curious scene. I put a small daypack on my back, stuffed a few items into the rear of the kayak, and pushed off into the gentle current at 8:30 am. This was near the headwaters of the Montréal River, and the flow was just large enough to navigate. I was alone, but I felt a great sense of contentment and control. The peace and quiet of the river was disturbed only by the soft gurgle of my paddle sweeping through the water.

Around a bend in the river I came across a huge bull moose and his cow. He was standing in the water and wasn't about to move. The river here was only a few metres wide, and I was nervous about going by so close. It occurred to me that this wasn't a good time of year to be challenging a bull moose for his cow.

"Okay big fella," I said as I approached, "yes, she's lovely, but she's all yours!" He snorted defiantly as I slowly drifted past.

Just before noon I came to Smoothwater Lake. I had heard that, contrary to its name, it can be very rough, and that people had drowned after capsizing on it. But Smoothwater Lake was true that day, and I paddled straight across to my first portage at the south end.

The first portage was 760 metres (2493 ft.) over a height of land to Apex Lake, so named because it is a watershed divide. Water to the north and east of Apex Lake follows the Montréal River drainage and those waters to the south flow into the Sturgeon River. I put my daypack on my back, my kayak on one shoulder, and started across. I had to rest a few times, and was wiped when I finally reached Apex Lake.

The short paddle across Apex Lake was only a brief respite. The next portage was 1100 metres (3609 ft.) over another height of land to a small unnamed lake. The portage seemed to go on forever, but I finally reached the other side. I crossed two more small lakes and two short portages before I finally arrived at the place where a campsite was marked on my map, only there was no campsite. But I was too tired to go any farther. I was carrying no tent in order to save weight, and just stretched a light nylon tarp between two trees for shelter. I had travelled 20 kilometres (12.5 mi.) since morning. A crimson sunset lit up the sky as I settled down for supper and a well-earned rest. As I drifted off to sleep, I felt in wonderful harmony with the wild and beautiful land around me. I recalled the words from one

The author's homemade kayak at the portage at the south end of Smoothwater Lake, Ontario.

of my favourite Robert Service poems, "...Here by the camp fire's flicker, deep in my blanket curled, I long for the peace of the pine-gloom, when the scroll of the Lord is unfurled...."

I awoke the next day, September 27, at 7:00 am, and was on the water paddling south shortly after 8:00 am. If all went well, this would be the day when I finished the Canadian highpoints. I crossed two more short portages, paddled across McCulloch Lake, and into Mihell Lake. Here, somewhere along the western shore, I needed to find the entrance to Scarecrow Creek. Finally I spotted it, but it was not at all what I expected. It was a tiny flow of water that I could barely navigate, even in my little kayak. Beaver dams often blocked the creek, and sometimes the alders growing out from the shores left almost no space to pass. The creek meandered back and forth, and seemed to last forever. I knew that paddling back up this creek later in the day would be an extremely difficult chore. But finally I emerged onto Scarecrow Lake, and my objective, Ishpatina Ridge, rose 300 metres (1000 ft.) above me.

A pile of logs on the right-hand shore marked the location of an old warden cabin and the trailhead. I had come about seven kilometres (4.3 mi.) from my camp in three hours. I pulled the kayak up on the shore and found the old trail leading five kilometres (3 mi.) to the top of Ishpatina Ridge. The trail

The summit of Ishpatina Ridge in 1997. This was the last of the original 12 Canadian highpoints to be climbed by the author.

was overgrown, but not difficult to follow. It climbed steadily through old-growth forest, past a small unnamed lake, then past Dick Lake, which was even smaller. Finally the trail broke out of the trees and an enormous fire tower came into view. The top of the ridge was mostly bedrock, covered with blueberry bushes and dwarf scrub oak. I stepped onto the highest point and basked in the sunshine of my accomplishment. I had climbed the 12 highpoints of Canada in five years, 115 days.

The view was memorable. A patchwork of lakes and hills spread out at my feet in all directions. I looked off about two kilometres (1.25 mi.) to the northeast where another crest of Ishpatina Ridge rose about as tall as the one where I stood. Both of these humps have a closed contour interval of 2250 feet on the topographic map. It's impossible to tell which of these humps is actually higher. I reasoned that the fire tower would be built on the highest one, and this was supported by an old book, *Temagami Canoe Routes*, published in 1979. On the other hand, the fire tower may have been located here mainly for convenience. Still, according to the information I had, this was the highest point, and it was here that my journey would end.

I showed marvellous restraint and resisted the temptation to climb the fire tower. The tower was obviously in very bad repair, and a sign read "DO NOT CLIMB," no doubt good advice. After a leisurely lunch on the summit, I started back down the trail. The paddle back to my camp was routine, except for the exhausting struggle up Scarecrow Creek, which alone took two hours. I paddled into camp at 5:00 pm, nine hours after leaving it in the morning. I went to sleep with only the calling of loons to break the silence of the wilderness.

The next morning I packed up and started back across the long portages toward home. But when I reached Smoothwater Lake, it had totally changed. A stiff wind blew from the south, and far out on the lake I could see big whitecaps breaking across the water. I wondered if I should take the short route straight across the lake, or sneak cautiously along the shore. I decided to go straight across, but soon regretted the decision. The waves, now coming from behind me, were huge. Paddling was tricky business. Sometimes a large wave caught the kayak, and I would surf ahead, riding its crest at breakneck speed. I knew that if the bow of the kayak were to bury in the trough between the waves, the kayak might turn quickly and roll. Of course, if the kayak had rolled, I could have, in theory, simply swept my paddle through the water and rolled up again. But my Eskimo roll was rusty at best, and in this surf, with a pack on my back, I had zero confidence in my ability to complete the manoeuvre. It was with great relief that I finally entered the shelter of the Montréal River on the far side of the Smoothwater Lake. I reached the Beauty Lake Road and my car at 3:30 pm.

The next day a dreary, steady rain set in for the drive home. I turned off Highway 11 at Burks Falls, Ontario, and headed west on a small paved road. I had been planning this diversion for some time. Just a few kilometres ahead was Lake Cecebe, where my father took me every summer as a child. In my mind's eye I could still picture the little rustic cabin and smell the aroma of sawdust and pine. At last I saw the lake ahead through the rain and fog. The little store where my sister and I used to row for candy and treats was gone. I turned left down the once-familiar old lane toward the cabins. But the cabins too were gone. In their place were tidy vacation homes with flower boxes and manicured lawns. I searched in vain for some sign of what used to be there nearly 50 years ago, but nothing was left aside from my own fond memories. I turned my car around in the rain and headed south again, toward Mary Fran and Jenny and home. Ahead of me lay new experiences and adventures, new mountains to climb. Specifically, I had discovered that Canada had formed a new territory called Nunavut, and that my Canadian highpointing days were not, in fact, over!

The High North

The nameless men who nameless rivers travel,
And in strange valleys greet strange deaths alone;
The grim, intrepid ones who would unravel
The mysteries that shroud the Polar Zone.

I leaned back in the plush seat of the Air Canada jet winging its way from Fort Nelson to Vancouver, British Columbia. It was July of 1993, just after our ill-fated attempt to climb Mount Nirvana, and I was scheduled to make a presentation at a business conference in Seattle. But my mind was not on the conference. Our failure to reach the summit of Mount Nirvana had been a bitter disappointment, and I was already beginning to plan another attempt. Perhaps if we approached the mountain from the east instead of the north?

I removed the airline magazine from the seat pocket and began to browse. Toward the back of the pamphlet was a small article about a new territory being formed in the Canadian Arctic. What! I sat upright with a start. The new territory was called "Nunavut," a word that means "our land" in the language of the aboriginal people, the Inuit, who make up the majority of its population. The small article said that the new territory was being carved from the Northwest Territories, but didn't say exactly where it was. I knew that both Baffin Island and Ellesmere Island in the Canadian Arctic bristled with rugged mountains nearly as high as Nirvana. Perhaps the new highpoint would be there. In any case, a new territory would have a new highpoint to climb, and I knew I would be going. As it turned out, the highpoint of Nunavut was even more exotic and compelling than I could have imagined.

Nearly five years later I anxiously tore open the letter from Greg Walker, the chief warden of Ellesmere Island National Park Reserve. Nearly every source at my disposal confirmed that the highest point of Nunavut was Barbeau Peak, a remote mountain that rises over the ice cap of Ellesmere

Looking northeast across the ice cap from the summit of Barbeau Peak. Photo Tony Daffern.

Island to 2670 metres (8760 ft.). But there was still a problem. The exact location and identity of Barbeau Peak was in dispute. The mountain was first climbed in 1967 by a party led by Geoffrey Hattersley-Smith, who later reported its location as 81°55' N, 75°02' W. But Allan Errington, who made the second ascent of the mountain, published a map in the *American Alpine Journal* that clearly showed Barbeau Peak to be at 81°54' N, 75°18' W. The two locations were nearly six kilometres (3.7 mi.) apart. Errington had named the mountain at the coordinates published by Hattersley-Smith "Victory." I located Allan Errington's name and phone number in the membership directory of the American Alpine Club and phoned him. "Oh there's no doubt," Allan proclaimed. "When you stand on the summit of Barbeau, you'll know it's the highest. And the summit register is there. Hattersley-Smith just got the location wrong." He seemed very confident. But Greg Walker's letter echoed my confusion. "We concur with your analysis," he began. "The exact location of Barbeau Peak is uncertain. We would be grateful if your expedition could resolve the issue." Even more remarkable, page 26 of the *Planet Earth MacMillan World Atlas*, a very respected publication, showed a mysterious unnamed peak several kilometres to the west at 2743 metres (8999 ft.), much higher than Barbeau Peak. Although this mysterious elevation would later prove to be nonexistent, I was amazed that the identity and location of such prominent peaks could still be in doubt.

Another Parks Canada brochure accompanying the letter from the chief warden proudly proclaimed Barbeau Peak to be "the highest point in eastern North America." So it was with considerable uncertainty that I began to organize a 1998 expedition to climb the highpoint of Nunavut. It would not be an easy task, or an inexpensive one. Ellesmere Island can be reached only by chartering a flight from the remote outpost of Resolute in the Northwest Territories. The round-trip cost of a twin engine Otter flight from Resolute to Ellesmere Island was about CAN $20,000. I would have to find several other climbers to share the cost, or I simply wouldn't be able to afford it.

Tom was committed to classes during the summer of 1998, but Dan quickly signed up for the trip. Tony Daffern, who accompanied me the previous year to Québec, also joined and enlisted Pete Ford, a climber friend of his from Canmore, Alberta. I was able to recruit a few others by posting an ad in the Highpointer's Club newsletter, and soon had an able crew of eight climbers signed up. The cost of the trip was suddenly reasonable.

The logistics of reaching the highpoint were daunting. The only landing strips in the national park were at Lake Hazen and Tanquary Fiord, both nearly 80 kilometres (50 mi.) away from Barbeau Peak. On the other hand, if we scheduled the expedition early enough, we could make a ski landing on the ice cap only a few kilometres from our objective, climb the mountain, then fly home. But then we would miss the famous flora and fauna of Ellesmere Island. Finally, a compromise plan emerged. We would land on the ice cap on June 14, identify the highpoint and climb it, then travel over the ice cap, down the Air Force Glacier, and across the tundra to Tanquary Fiord. The terrain and the difficulties were largely unknown to us, but the plan looked good. The remaining uncertainties only added to my excitement as the trip approached.

It was late at night, June 12, 1998, when Dan and I finally arrived at the Nisku Inn outside the Edmonton airport. Several other members of our expedition had arrived earlier in the day, but we didn't bother to rouse them. We were more interested in two packages from the University of Calgary. The packages contained cross-country skis and boots. Dan and I were both competent skiers and wanted to ski across the ice cap of Ellesmere Island, but we didn't have suitable skis or ski boots. Nor could we rent such specialized equipment in Ohio. So, with the help of Pete Ford from Canmore, we arranged to rent equipment from the University of Calgary and have it shipped to us at the Nisku Inn. This was a risk. If the boots didn't fit, there would be no time to make an exchange before flying north to Resolute.

Once in our room, we eagerly tore open the boxes and tried on the boots. Disaster! Dan's boots were too tight, and I couldn't even force my feet into mine. The extra pair of boots, which I had sent as a precaution, were also too tight. But I found that by taking off my wool socks, and using only thin liner socks, that I could just barely stuff my feet into the heavy boots. It worked for Dan too. So, after stomping around in the parking lot for a few minutes, we both decided that the boots would do despite being uncomfortably snug. We didn't expect to encounter very cold temperatures, and the double plastic boots would provide just enough insulation without heavy socks. They would have to do.

After a few hours of sleep we went down to breakfast, and to meet the other members of our expedition. Climbers, most of whom had never met each other, were assembling here from six states and the province of Alberta. It was fascinating to meet each other after several months of communication by phone and email. I was most anxious to meet Tom Budlong from California, as Tom was tenting with Dan and me. Climbers are not usually hard to pick out in a crowd. They often wear heavy Vibram-soled hiking boots, and their clothing is best described as "unconventional." They have a rough look about them. But Tom Budlong was an exception. He was lean, grandfatherly-looking and walked with a cane. A cane! Later in the morning I saw him walking with two canes! But his appearance belied a strong and determined character. Tom was a 61 year-old semi-retired mechanical engineer and computer professional from Los Angeles. He was an expert on the Inyo Mountains of Southern California, and spent every opportunity exploring their steep terrain, rediscovering forgotten mining trails and artifacts. This, and other treks in the American southwest, had made him hard as nails.

Three other climbers also introduced themselves that morning. Greg Slayden was a friendly 34 year-old highpointer from Seattle who had climbed all 50 US highpoints, as well as 25 highpoints of other countries. Greg was a computer cartographer for Microsoft, and possessed a wealth of geographic information. He could talk endlessly in detail about mountains, time zones and all kinds of geographical trivia, and make it all sound fascinating.

River crossings can be a major problem in the Canadian Arctic. Tom Budlong crossing a braid of the Rollrock River. Photo Tony Daffern.

Bill Salter was a 47 year-old vice president for the Central Michigan Railway. Bill had also climbed all 50 US highpoints, as well as the high Mexican volcanoes, and had made an attempt on Aconcagua, the highest mountain in the western hemisphere. Bill had a quiet and unassuming manner, and was instantly likeable.

The final member of the expedition at the Nisku Inn was Dave Rotheroe, a 33 year-old manager for Hewlett Packard in computer systems. Dave had climbed 49+ US highpoints, having reached the 5242-metre (17,200 ft.) level on Mount McKinley, and had hiked most of the trails in the Grand Canyon. Dave seemed a little brash and full of confidence for the climb ahead.

After breakfast we loaded a jumble of gear and equipment into the Nisku van for a shuttle to the airport. Onlookers wondered where we could be going with skis, sleds, boots, duffels and heavy packs. But eventually we managed to get it all checked aboard Canadian North flight 446 bound for Yellowknife, Cambridge Bay and finally Resolute. At the departure gate we met the last two members of our expedition, Tony Daffern and his friend Pete Ford.

Tony and I already knew each other, as we had travelled and tented together the year before in Québec, but I had never before met Pete Ford. Pete looked like a hermit just roused from some cabin in the backwoods. He had a scraggly beard and long blond hair, which was tied up in a knot behind his head. He was 61 years old, a retired physics specialist from the University of Edmonton. He was of English background, and had an amiable but somewhat irascible personality. Pete's slight build disguised a tough and stubborn climber. He had already climbed the East Ridge of Mount Logan, Chimborazo in Ecuador, and the Aquiline Nose of Mount Christie. Pete had also been to the southern Logan Mountains near Mount Nirvana and struggled through the mosquitoes and brush along the Flat River, not once or twice, but three times! This, more than anything else, was ample testimony to his dogged determination.

So the motley expedition was together at last, and we eagerly boarded the plane for the long flight north. The first stop was Yellowknife in the Northwest Territories. Yellowknife was a lovely remote village on the shores of Great Slave Lake. This would be our last look at forests and familiar vegetation. The next stop was the lonely mining outpost of Cambridge Bay. We had a little time on the ground in Cambridge Bay, so I decided to get out and walk around. I was stunned! There were no trees, shrubs or any apparent vegetation to soften the stark landscape. A cold, harsh wind blew off the ice-covered sea. I remember thinking, "You ain't in Kansas anymore dearie!" And we still had to fly another 800 kilometres (500 mi.) north to Resolute.

Two hours later the plane was circling over the dusty airstrip outside Resolute. The landscape didn't look any more inviting than it had at Cambridge Bay. Off to the east, across the Wellington Channel, I could just make out the southwest shore of Devon Island. This was a place of legendary hardship. In 1845, the ships Erebus and Terror of the Franklin expedition sailed into the channel in an effort to find the elusive Northwest Passage. After being stopped by ice, Franklin returned and spent the winter of 1845-6 on

Beechey Island, a tiny spit of land off the coast of Devon Island. The following spring Franklin continued southwest on his fatal quest. The ships and all hands were never heard from again. Presumably the ships were locked in the relentless ice and those on board starved to death. Remains of Franklin's wintering were later found on Beechey Island, which became an important depot and meeting place for future expeditions searching for his remains. Roald Amundson also passed through Resolute Bay when he finally negotiated the Northwest Passage in 1903-6.

After landing, the tiny airport building became a mob scene of people gathering gear and making contact with adventure and charter flight companies. Resolute was the jumping-off point for expeditions to both the north magnetic and geographic poles, as well as Ellesmere Island. Tony and Pete had decided to stay overnight at the Qausuittuq Inn before our flight to Ellesmere Island the next day. At the last minute, Greg and Dave decided to join them. But the going rate at the Qausuittuq Inn was $185 per person per night—too rich for my blood. I wasn't that desperate yet. So I located Morag Howell, the base manager for First Air. Morag was a small red-haired woman with a strong Scottish brogue. "Can't we just sack out here in the terminal or in your air cargo hanger?" I asked. "Oh no!" she replied. "You can't do that. Just sleep anywhere outside the airport grounds. You needn't go far."

So while half of our group went off to soft, albeit expensive, beds for the night, the rest of us looked for a good spot to put up our tents. It wasn't easy. The ground was generally rocky and unfriendly. But there was one soft green patch of turf just below the airport, and here we set up for the night. After a little dinner, we tried to adjust to sleeping in the glare of airport lights—not an easy task.

The next morning we were walking back toward the airport when the driver of a pickup truck stopped to give us a little friendly advice. "Don't camp in that green area over there." He warned, pointing to where we had just camped. "That's the raw sewage outlet for the whole airport." I could only reply, "Oh shit!"

Back in the First Air cargo hanger, we sorted gear and supplies for the adventure ahead. The weather forecast for our landing on Ellesmere Island was good. We boarded the twin engine Otter on June 14 at 10:00 am for the long four-hour flight north. At first thick clouds obscured the land, but eventually gave way to crystal clear skies. As we approached Ellesmere Island, we could see the Innuitian Mountains shining white in the distance. I was quietly relieved. If bad weather had prevented us from landing on the ice cap, the whole expedition could have been foiled.

We landed at Tanquary Fiord to take on fuel. Tanquary Fiord is a narrow finger of sea and ice probing deep into the island. The fiord was still frozen, and hanging glaciers draped the steep mountainsides above. A warden office and a few small buildings huddled at the end of the runway. If all went well we would land on the ice cap, climb Barbeau Peak, and come hiking back to Tanquary Fiord 13 days later.

National park headquarters at Tanquary Fiord. Photo Tony Daffern.

After a brief time on the ground, we were on our way up the Air Force River valley. This was the route we intended to take back to Tanquary Fiord, and we eagerly searched the ground to see what would lie in store for us. Getting off the glacier onto the land looked especially tough. The toe of the glacier was a 20 metre-high (65 ft.) wall of ice with no easy exit.

I looked ahead as the highest peaks came into view. Our pilot, Amy, had never before landed on the north side of the range. But the peaks are more gradual on the north, and it was there that we needed to be. Amy first flew alongside the high range of peaks. But which was the highest? There were three peaks only about four kilometres (2.5 mi.) apart that all looked about the same height. "I think the sharp one in the centre is highest," I said. "My money's on the big one to the west," said someone else. Even now the exact identity of Barbeau Peak was still a mystery. Amy turned the Twin Otter and flew back along the ridge. We still couldn't tell which was highest.

Amy then turned her attention to locating a landing site. She flew north, carefully checking the ice cap for signs of hidden crevasses. There didn't appear to be any. She touched the Otter down, making long tracks in the snow, and lifted off again. She flew back across the landing site, again checking for crevasses. This was no place to make a mistake. Finally she touched down on the tracks she had made and slowly came to a stop. We were down, and only about 11 kilometres (6.8 mi.) northwest of Barbeau Peak. After we unloaded our gear and supplies, the Otter turned, took off, and disappeared into the clear blue sky.

I felt a wave of relief. The uncertainties about the weather and the landing site were behind us, and we were within striking distance of our goal. We were at last alone in this exquisite arctic wilderness. The ice beneath our feet crept slowly north toward the M'Clintock Inlet and the Arctic Ocean. Mount Oxford and Mount Whisler rose in lonely isolation to the east. Mount Whisler, only a little lower than Barbeau Peak, was first sighted and reported by Lieutenant Adolphus Greely from Lake Hazen during one of his inland excursions in 1881-3. Greely led a US Army expedition to Ellesmere Island in 1881, intent upon establishing an American claim in the arctic islands. He established Fort Conger on the northeast shore of the island in 1881. But supply ships were unable to penetrate the sea ice for two summers, and Greely ordered a general retreat south in August of 1883. They didn't get far. The party, weak from hardship, hunger and chronic bronchitis, established a dismal starvation camp on Pim Island where 18 out of 25 perished. How ironic that this, as well as other tragedies in the Arctic, occurred in a land where the native Inuit people not only survived, but flourished.

We were at an elevation of about 1500 metres (5000 ft.), lower down than I had hoped, but close enough for a summit attempt. We quickly erected our tents and made a comfortable camp in beautiful weather. Tony and Pete were concerned that the good weather wouldn't last, and were anxious to make a summit attempt immediately. So, after a brief rest, Tony and Pete, joined by Greg, set off for Barbeau Peak at about 8:00 pm. The rest of us decided to wait until the next morning.

The next morning the weather was still brilliant, and we made preparations for our climb. I was concerned that Tony, Pete and Greg were not back yet. They had been gone nearly 12 hours and were nowhere in sight. What could have happened? Tom, Bill and Dave put on snowshoes, roped together, and started trudging off in the tracks leading toward the peaks. Dan and I stepped into our skis and followed them a few minutes later. It was nearly 8:30 am.

After we had gone only a few hundred metres, Dan shouted, "Look, there they are!" Three tiny specks, moving fast across a steep slope, appeared to the left of the mountain ahead. What a relief! Soon we were together and Tony was telling us about their climb. After ascending the valley above our camp, they reached a high saddle and realized that the mountain ahead was probably not Barbeau Peak. So they descended about 100 metres (330 ft.), crossed a small cirque, then climbed up to the west ridge of the peak they reckoned to be Barbeau. Greg put on his crampons and attempted to climb the west ridge, but soon found himself on steep, hard ice, and retreated down the ridge. All three then made a perilous traverse across steep ice to reach the north ridge of the peak. The way up from there looked easier, but they were tired and a little intimidated by the ice they had just crossed. Nevertheless, after a brief rest they continued up and reached the summit at about 6:00 am. There they found the register left by the first ascent party, and confirmed that they were indeed on the highest point. The three men then descended the valley to the east of the one they went up, and intercepted us. "Follow the tracks we left on the way down," Tony advised, "and you'll save yourself a load of trouble." We were happy to oblige. Even so, the day would not be easy. We had about 1100

Above: Dan Bennett on the summit ridge.
Right: Final approach to Barbeau Peak with the sharp summit ridge ahead.

metres (3600 ft.) to ascend, and nearly 24 kilometres (15 mi.) to travel up and back.

The grade was not difficult. We gradually ascended a series of moderate snow slopes until at last the summit of Barbeau Peak came into view. It was indeed the small summit I had spotted from the Otter on our flight in. After crossing a long flat area, we started up the slope leading to the north ridge. Here Dave's leg disappeared into a rare crevasse. This was not a place entirely without danger. Travelling on skis is safer in a crevasse field, and Dan and I kept our skis on until we were only about 50 metres (160 ft.) below the peak. Here we switched to crampons for the final steep slope to the summit.

The final summit ridge was sharp and airy, soaring into the chilly arctic sky. It was a worthy highpoint for the remarkable new territory of Nunavut. Dan and I stepped onto the summit of my last Canadian highpoint June 15 at 2:00 pm, and Tom, Dave and Bill soon followed. We had brought levels to confirm that this was the highest summit, and after careful checking there was no doubt. The view was fantastic. Icy mountains stretched away in every direction. To the north, the land gave way to the arctic ice pack, all that remained between there and the geographic North Pole. Dan climbed down to a rocky outcrop on the south ridge, and found the summit register left by Hattersley-Smith after his first ascent. There also was the signature of Allan Errington. Errington had indeed climbed Barbeau Peak, but had mislocated it on the map he constructed and published in the *American Alpine Journal*. Tom took out his GPS device, acquired positioning satellites, and carefully took readings that correlated with readings taken earlier by Tony and Greg. The identity and location of the highest point in the Canadian Arctic would no longer be in question.

It was time to go down. And here the skis proved their worth. On the way up, those walking on snowshoes kept up with Dan and me. But going down, we cruised effortlessly, arriving back at camp by 4:45 pm. The walkers dragged in about an hour and a half later. Throughout the trip the skis proved to be a great asset while we were on the ice, and a big nuisance on the tundra when we had to load them on our backs.

After a well-earned rest, we considered what we should do next. It was a highly unusual dilemma. Usually we struggle for days to reach a summit, with only enough time remaining to hurry down. But now we had reached the summit on the first day of the expedition. True, we still had about 80 kilometres (50 mi.) of ice and tundra to cover in the next 12 days, but that still left us with extra time on our hands. Tony and Pete wanted to stay on the ice cap and climb some of the surrounding peaks. The rest of us wanted to head toward Tanquary Fiord, climb a peak or two along the way, and also spend time on the tundra. In the end Tony and Pete decided to head off with us toward the top of the Air Force Glacier, and the group remained intact.

We first had to climb up the ice cap and over a divide. The slope was gradual, but it seemed long to me. Perhaps the effort of the previous day was taking its toll. We made camp just at the top of the slope leading down toward the Air Force Glacier. Tony, Pete and Greg pushed on a bit farther, planning to climb a magnificent 2100 metre-high (7000 ft.) peak at the head of the glacier.

The next morning Dan, who was feeling more fit than I, skied up to join Tony, Pete and Greg for their ascent of the unnamed peak. Their climb of the peak, done completely on skis, took only about five hours. At the first summit they looked across to another hump that looked somewhat higher, but the wind was fierce. It whipped off Tony's hat, which disappeared off toward the DeVries Glacier. They decided to descend. Once everyone was back in camp, we packed up and headed down toward the Air Force River valley.

The next few days were memorable. Those of us on skis would glide quickly ahead, then rest while walkers caught up. I had decided to pull a bright red snow sled behind me to take weight off my back. Three others also pulled sleds, while four did not. Walking on the ice cap and glacier was easy. Crevasses were rare and the footing was firm. At one point Tom even walked out of his snowshoe, leaving it behind. He actually went several hundred metres before he noticed it missing. Tom took a lot of good-natured ribbing for this, and for his cane, which he continued to use even on the snow and ice. The arctic sun circled slowly around a clear blue sky. It never even approached the horizon. Each day brought a new view of the exquisite mountains and wilderness around us. Especially beautiful was a graceful snow-covered peak on our right. As we approached it, we saw that it was a prominent 1500+ metre-high peak (5000+ ft.) that split the glacier on which we were travelling. The ice to the right flowed into the DeVries Glacier, and ultimately north into the Arctic Ocean. The ice to the left of the peak continued south down the Air Force Glacier toward Tanquary Fiord. We decided to climb it.

On June 18 Dan and I broke camp and got an early start. We skied to the foot of the East Ridge of the peak and put on our crampons. The ridge was not steep at first, but the angle increased as we neared the east summit. This was no place to lose concentration. A careless step could have led to a long and possibly deadly slide down the south face. Beyond the east summit, a steep step and an exhilarating arête led to the highest point. Dan and I shared an embrace. What a privilege it was to share this moment with him. Had this peak been climbed before? Perhaps, but there was no way of knowing. The summit was completely snow-covered, with no place to leave a record of our passing. We huddled below the summit to escape the wind and enjoy the view. Unnamed summits and glaciers stretched toward the horizon on every side. Too soon it was time to turn our backs on the summit and descend to the valley below. Just below the east summit we met Tony, Pete, Greg and Bill coming up. All were in great spirits. We decided to name the mountain Highpointer Peak, and continued our descent down the glacier.

By the night of June 20 we were camped near the toe of the Air Force Glacier, and the glacier had turned from benign to threatening. On our right lay a menacing field of crevasses, and numerous meltwater channels crossed our path ahead. We also knew that a 20 metre-high (65 ft.) wall of ice barred our exit from the glacier.

In the morning we broke camp, shouldered our packs and headed toward the meltwater channels. These channels form in June when the surface of the glacier melts in the continuous sunshine. The channels gradually grow deeper and wider as the summer progresses. They can become very risky to cross. The first channels we encountered were narrow, and I could ski across them by gathering a little speed. But as we continued, the channels became larger and more menacing, and I had to search for a narrow point to cross. Once I was skiing alongside a swift channel searching for a narrow spot and not paying enough attention to my sled behind me. I glanced to my right and was horrified to see my sled, loaded with gear, floating down the channel past me! Only a quick rescue prevented my gear from getting soaked. Finally, as the channels became wider, Dan and I helped each other by throwing our gear across, then running and jumping over. Greg had the misfortune to fall into a channel and get thoroughly soaked. But finally we left the last meltwater channel behind us.

Pete Ford crossing a melt stream on the lower Air Force Glacier. Photo Tony Daffern.

Our exit from the glacier was easy. We had come down one of the few places where there was a smooth transition from ice to land. Only the Air Force River barred our way to dry tundra. Tony waded across straight away, which was his custom. I followed, but was shocked to find that the river bottom was smooth, slippery ice, and I was very nearly swept off my feet. It would have been a disaster if all my gear had become soaked in the icy water.

It was a delight to finally walk onto dry land and set up camp. Tiny flowers—purple saxifrage, arctic poppy and willow—bloomed in profusion. Just above our camp, the skeleton of a muskox gave stark testimony to the harshness of the land. How, I wondered, could these ancient animals survive the arctic winter? Muskox do not hibernate. When the icy darkness of winter comes, they huddle together and paw the ground for low willow and scrub. They have survived this way for millions of years.

The next few days were unforgettable. We moved slowly down the Air Force River valley, moving about 10 kilometres (6 mi.) between camps. There was plenty of time to relish the scenery around us and to take side trips to Ekblaw Lake and up the Rollrock River. The weather was lovely. Our only disappointment was the absence of muskox, though a few had been seen in the valley a few days before. We hiked into the national park outpost at Tanquary Fiord on June 26. Here we were treated to a bunkhouse with eight beds, a cookhouse and a visitor centre, all for us. The outpost gets 60-70 visitors per year, but most come later in the summer.

The next day, park wardens Greg Walker and Liasa Audaluk took us on a tour of Independence-I, the ruins of an Inuit village near Kettle Lake. It was difficult to imagine that the ancient stone rings and fox traps before us were 4000 years old; as old as the pyramids of Egypt. The culture of the Inuit remained almost unchanged until the European explorers discovered it in the 18th century. I found myself wondering what life was like for those people in this harsh and beautiful land. They must have been resourceful and skilled beyond belief. We took an enjoyable hike up a nearby mountain, then down through Green Valley, and suddenly it was time to go. We flew back to

Campsite near the toe of the Air Force Glacier.

Resolute June 28 to revel in hot showers and home-cooked food. By then the $185 per person charge at the Qausuittuq Inn seemed like a bargain.

I had taken five years, 361 days to climb all 13 Canadian highpoints. Later, Pete chided me. "This whole idea of list-keeping and climbing highpoints is completely foreign to me," he scoffed. "I have a friend that won't even admit to continuing to the summit after a good rock climb!" But I'm sure that even Pete's friend has a list of rock climbs he cherishes. The top of the rock is his goal just as the summit is mine. The difficulty of very technical rock and ice climbing has left me far behind, but I can still delight in the joy and wonder of high places. The delight that these wild and extraordinary highpoints has given me is real. Each and every Canadian highpoint, like patchwork in a beautiful quilt, will forever have a place in my memory and my heart.

Mount Logan

Yukon Territory

5957 m (19,545 ft.)
Lat/long N60° 34' 00" W140° 24' 10"
UTM 532750m.E. 6714600m.N. (NAD 27)
Topo maps 115 C/9 McArthur Peak
and 115 C/10 King Peak

Mount Logan is quite possibly the largest mountain on earth. Its huge massif looms like a gigantic landlocked iceberg barely 80 km (50 mi.) from the Pacific Ocean. It is the second highest mountain above its base in the world. Mount Logan rises from the largest icefield outside the polar regions, a 70,000 sq. km (44,000 sq. mi.) wilderness of ice and snow astride the border between Alaska and the Yukon Territory of Canada. A full 65 sq. km (40 sq. mi.) of Mount Logan's colossal summit plateau rises above 5000 m (16,400 ft.). A secondary mountain range, spectacular in its own right, towers above the summit plateau with no less than eight distinct summits. Where other mountains may create an image of beauty or symmetry, Mount Logan leaves an overwhelming impression of scale, impregnability and intimidation.

The massive Saint Elias Mountain Range rises along the northeastern shore of the Gulf of Alaska. The 16 highest mountains in Canada are all in the Saint Elias Mountains, and all but one of these are wholly within the Yukon Territory. Compressive and shearing forces produced by movements between the Pacific plate and the North American plate created several fault lines, one of which traverses the lower part of the south face and ridges of Mount Logan. This fault, called the Border Ranges Fault, caused the sedimentary rocks in the south to pile up or slide under the granite rocks to the south. When molten and granite rocks to the north of the fault were forced to rise up, and the overlying strata was stripped off by erosion, Mount Logan was born. Today, Mount Logan is still rising. The snow and ice that cover the top of the giant mountain may be thousands of years old where it lies in contact with the rock 200-300 m (600-1000 ft.) below the surface.

The Saint Elias Mountains were named in the late 1800s after Mount Saint Elias, a name originally bestowed by the Danish explorer Vitus Bering on Saint Elias Day in 1741. When the United States purchased Alaska in 1867, most of its coastal regions had been charted, but little was known of its vast inland territory. During his second expedition to Mount Saint Elias in 1891, Israel Russell reached a high col at 4400 m (14,400 ft.). "What met my eager gaze," he wrote, "was a vast snow-covered region, limitless in its expanse, through which hundreds, and perhaps thousands, of barren angular mountain-peaks projected."[1] He named the gigantic massif to the north "Mount Logan," after Sir William Logan, the founder and first director of the Geological Survey of Canada. Mount Logan remained in lonely isolation until 1925, 12 years after the first ascent of Mount McKinley.

The first ascent of Mount Logan was perhaps the most extraordinary epic of hardship and endurance in the annals of North American mountaineering. It was a hardy group of eight climbers that gathered in the little Alaskan town of McCarthy early in May of 1925. The party included Allen Carpé and Andrew Taylor, who would later make the first ascent of Mount Fairweather. Their challenge was to negotiate on foot a 160 km (100 mi.) march up the Chatina River, then nearly 100 km (60 mi.) of glaciers and the 5000 m (16,000 ft.) of altitude that separated them from the summit of Mount Logan.

After 19 days of backbreaking effort, more than two tons of supplies had been brought to base camp at nearly 2500 m (8000 ft.) on the Ogilvie Glacier. Another move up to Observation camp at 3000 m (9800 ft.) and the climbers could finally look south to where Mount Saint Elias loomed in lonely dignity across the icefields. Here the climbers entered the King Trench, the high glacial valley between Logan and the Matterhorn-like spire of King Peak.

Allen Carpé described King Col as one of their most enjoyable camps. Here he relates an "…indescribable keenness and exhilaration that comes from the heights. It seemed to me that my senses were quickened and every moment lived twice. The cold and the wind and the thinness of the air did not let us forget that we were embarking now into a region where men cannot live long, and that a very few days must decide the outcome."[2] From King Col the pioneers struggled to find their way onto the great summit plateau of Mount Logan.

Allen Carpé and his weary party then climbed the prominent double pinnacle above, assuming this to be their goal. But when they arrived, another summit loomed higher to the east. Already weakened by toil and the elements, they headed into the valley, toward the peak still above them. Said Carpé, "…we had gone through too much to give in now, although it was clear that we could not get back to camp that night if we went on." They finally reached the true summit at 8 pm of June 23. As Carpé described it, "…a narrow edge of ice soared into the thin fog above us, as slender and exposed as any Alpine summit. It was a noble culmination for the great mountain."[2]

It was the dreadful descent from the summit that earned Allen Carpé and his party a place in the pages of North American mountaineering, and very nearly cost them their lives. Too weak to retrace their steps over the west peak, they tried instead to circle around it and intercept the marked trail on the other side. Finally, with the light failing, and with little notion of where they were, they scooped shallow holes in the snow and lay down for the night. The next morning their situation was desperate. They had to move, despite poor weather and their weakened condition. Lambert's feet were freezing. At last, with a shout of relief, they chanced to find one of the thin willow twigs that marked their ascent trail. But the weather was so dense that they lost the trail again and became separated. Three of the party miraculously stumbled upon the tents, but Carpé and three others staggered on through another night, during which the thermometer read -32°C (-25°F). At one point they regained the willow trail, but followed it the wrong way on the featureless plateau before realizing their error. After 42 hours without shelter, Carpé and his companions cut off their frozen clothing and crawled exhausted into their sleeping bags.

The next day, in a race to escape the fearful plateau, they fought through a raging storm to find the trail through the pass and onto the slopes below. By the time they reached the relative safety of King Col they were fantastic figures indeed. "Great icicles hung from our beards and noses, our eyes were frozen shut. The mat of ice that covered McCarthy's face was crimson with blood. Lambert's feet were frozen and he was almost blind."[2] In the end the entire party returned safely to McCarthy, Alaska.

Mount Logan was not climbed again until 1950, when the second and third ascents were made on the original 1925 route. The East Ridge of Mount Logan was first climbed in 1957, and the remarkable Hummingbird Ridge, the dominant feature of the south face of Mount Logan, was climbed in 1965. Although 13 different routes have now been pioneered on the mountain, the King Trench and the East Ridge routes together account for 95 per cent of the recent ascents of Mount Logan.

Mount Logan is closely regulated today. It is necessary to register all expeditions with the wardens at Kluane National Park. Expeditions must consist of not less than four climbers, and each climber must submit a physician's certificate and a full resume of his mountain climbing experience. A complete plan for the climb must be submitted, including the expedition's route plan, schedule, personal equipment, group equipment and menu. Proof must be offered of radio support. Finally, it is necessary to check in with the wardens at Haines Junction before embarking on the climb. This is also a good opportunity to check on local conditions and weather forecasts. Such precautions are certainly justified by Mount Logan's remoteness and severe weather.

The most popular months of ascent are April through June. Tremendous snowfall (the roar of avalanches is a constant companion), high winds and cold (-40° even in June) can be expected at all elevations and at any time of the year. Rescue, although possible, is not easily or quickly arranged in the Wrangle-Saint Elias Range.

King Trench

The standard modern-day approach is to land on the Quintino-Sella Glacier at about 2700 m (9000 ft.) and climb north into the King Trench, joining the same route pioneered by Carpé in 1925 near Observation camp. This remains the easiest route to the summit, and in recent years, about 70 per cent of the climbers on Mount Logan have chosen to ascend the King Trench.

Charter flights may be arranged from Kluane Lake (Icefield Ranges Expeditions), Yukon Territory, from Yakutat, Alaska (Gulf Air Taxi), or from the Chitina River, northeast of Valdez, Alaska (Ultima Thule Outfitters). Charter services are also available based in Whitehorse, but this makes for a much longer charter flight. Climbers should compare all options for the best price and convenience.

To fly in with Icefield Ranges Expeditions from Kluane Lake, first take a scheduled commercial flight to Whitehorse, Yukon Territory. The landing strip at Kluane Lake is about 220 km (135 mi.) west of Whitehorse on the Alaskan Highway. A car can be rented in Whitehorse for the drive, or a ride may be arranged with the charter service. The airstrip at Kluane Lake is about 130 km (80 mi.) from Mount Logan.

To fly in from the Chitina River, arrangements can be made with Ultima Thule Outfitters for a five- to six-hour ride from Anchorage to a landing strip northeast of Valdez. From here passengers are flown to the Claus family lodge on the Chatina River. Paul Claus flies climbers in a single engine Beaver from the lodge to Mount Logan, about 200 km (125 mi.) away.

Gulf Air Taxi flies climbers to Mount Logan from Yakutat, Alaska. Yakutat is serviced by Alaska Airlines twice daily, once northbound and once southbound, so reaching the charter airstrip is convenient. Yakutat is also the closest access point, being only about 100 km (60 mi.) from Mount Logan, but as it is on the coast, Yakutat probably has the least reliable flying weather.

The King Trench route normally begins with a landing on the Quintino-Sella Glacier at an elevation of about 2700 m (9000 ft.). The climb from the Quintino-Sella Glacier into the King Trench is straightforward, but is laced with crevasses. The usual approach is to stay to the right when entering the trench. A camp is usually placed at a large flat area located at 3380 m (11,100

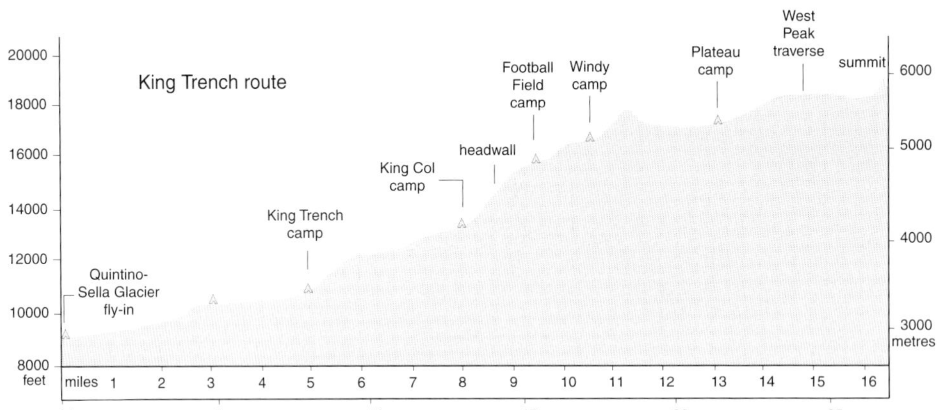

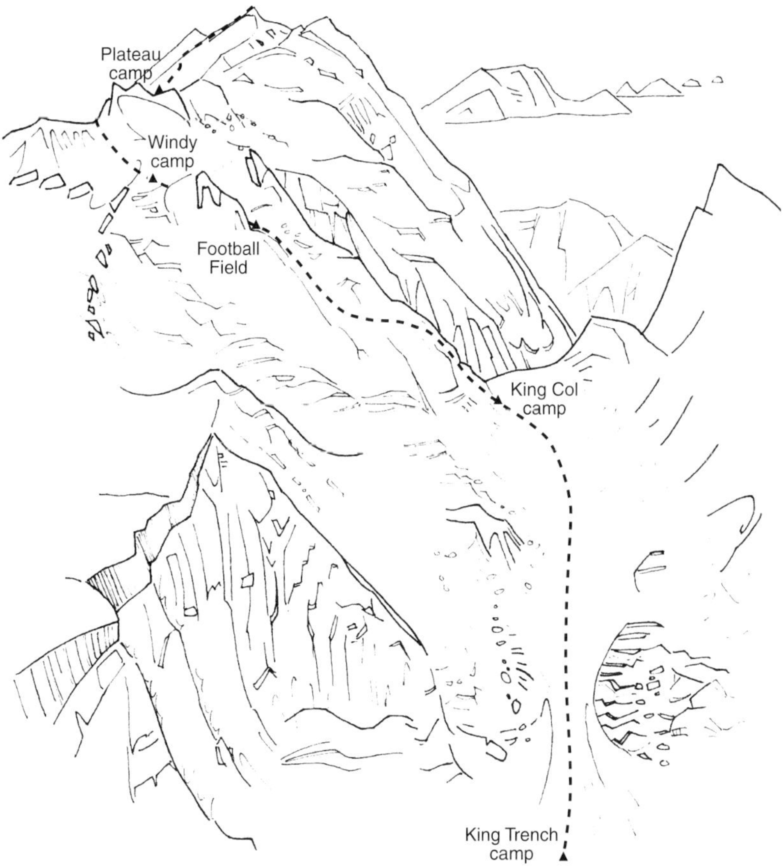

ft.). This is known as King Trench camp. It is also possible to glacier-land here, but the need to acclimatize makes a lower landing a better choice.

The next good campsite is at King Col, which is 730 m (2395 ft.) higher and 5 km (3 mi.) distant. It is not recommended to site a camp sooner as avalanches rumble almost continuously down the north face of King Peak. From King Trench camp, climb the icefall above. A relatively crevasse-free ramp leads up the centre of the icefall. The glacier flattens out at about 3800 m (12,500 ft.), but again, it is not recommended to camp here. Push on to King Col at 4120 m (13,500 ft.). It is reasonable to plan to reach King Col for the fifth night on the mountain.

Above King Col is the headwall, a 460 m-high (1500 ft.) 45° slope that many consider the crux of the route. Unconsolidated snow may avalanche from this slope. The headwall and the terrain above it up to nearly 5200 m (17,000 ft.) are heavily crevassed, and extreme precautions should be taken here against a crevasse fall. The best route from King Col up to the Football Field, a large flat area at 4900 m (16,000 ft.), will vary from year to year depending on the location of the crevasses, and one must simply find a path through the icefalls and seracs.

Mount Logan from the west showing the King Trench, the slopes up to King Col and the much foreshortened route to the summit. Note that the true summit is not visible in this photograph. Photo Walter Wood, courtesy Arctic Institute of North America.

The next obvious campsite above King Col is Football Field camp, but several other possibilities exist for smaller campsites along the way. One strategy is to make a carry-up from King Col as high as can be managed, then the next day to move camp all the way from King Col camp to Football Field camp, a taxing increase of 760 m (2500 ft.) in elevation.

From Football Field camp the route leads generally left through the icefalls to Windy camp at about 5200 m (17,000 ft.). Windy camp is the last large flat area before the slopes leading up to the summit plateau of Mount Logan. This was the camp from which Allen Carpé and his party made their last fateful push toward the summit of Mount Logan in 1925.

From Windy camp a moderate slope leads up to Iona Col, the 5500 m-high (18,000 ft.) gateway to Mount Logan's ice plateau. The notch leading left onto the plateau is almost the last feasible point before Prospector's Peak, the first in a line of several summits. It is usual to make a carry to the col and leave a cache, returning to Windy camp for a final night before heading onto the plateau.

From Windy camp it is a decisive move through the Iona Col and onto the great ice plateau. Once on the plateau, retreat involves a significant climb back up and through the col. It is sensible to climb to the cache at the col, pick up the cache, and pull sleds onto the plateau as the angle is generally flat or gradual. It is wise to push as far to the east on the plateau as possible to minimize the summit day. Plateau camp is likely to be at an altitude of about 5360 m (17,600 ft.) and about 5 km (3 mi.) from the true summit, which will still be hidden from view.

Some climbers ascend only the first peak (the west summit), and consider it good enough, being within 30 m (100 ft.) in elevation of the highest point. But nothing except the true summit will do for the purist.

From Plateau camp, head directly toward the twin-peaked west summit. Then, at an altitude slightly above 5500 m (18,000 ft.), traverse left around the north face of the west peak. The face is not very steep here, but is likely to be hard ice in places, and any fall must be arrested quickly. This traverse will finally bring the climber over a shoulder nearly level with the pass between the west peak and the true summit. Here the highest point of Mount Logan comes into view. Head into the pass, then traverse across the north face, heading for the notch between the east peak and the true summit. Here again the slope is not steep, but is likely to be icy.

Once in the notch, the true summit of Mount Logan is only a few metres away, but here lies the most difficult climbing of the route. It may be necessary to cut a few steps and belay the final steep step to the top. On a clear day the view from the top of Mount Logan is spectacular.

Return to Plateau camp, King Col and the Quintino-Sella Glacier by the same route in reverse. Getting a return charter flight back to civilization is often difficult as good weather must prevail both on the glacier and at the site of the charter airstrip. Such delays can be particularly frustrating at the end of a long, hard climb when food, supplies and patience run low.

East Ridge

Rising abruptly out of the 150 km-long (94 mi.) Hubbard Glacier, the East Ridge of Mount Logan is a classic and beautiful route second only to the King Trench in popularity. First ascended in 1957, this ridge now sees approximately 20 per cent of the total peak traffic.

This route is perhaps the "sanest" of Mount Logan's 13 odd ridges that provide access to the summit. The climbing experience on the route may be characterized best as a "hurry up and wait" scenario, interspersed with load carries over moderately technical terrain. Most of the climbing on the ridge will be on snow and ice, broken up by short rock bands. Climbers should expect difficulty in the range of 5.6 on short, 70° sections.

The commonly used campsites on the ridge are aesthetically situated and relatively safe with respect to avalanche hazard. Camps are usually located in the crest of the ridge, affording inspiring views. They are spacious enough for at least four large expedition tents per site.

Most parties will find a selection of ice screws, pickets and a small amount of rock gear useful. A mechanical ascender (useful as a running belay) in conjunction with up to three 50 m-long (164 ft.) ropes used as fixed lines will make the repeated ascent and descent on the short, steep sections between carries more tolerable. Shovels, of course, are indispensable.

Because of unstable and unpredictable weather, expedition-style climbing is the rule. Climbers plan for up to 20 days on the route and typically fly in with no less than 30 days' supply of food and fuel.

The ski plane drops climbers off on the Hubbard Glacier at 2000 m (6700 ft.) and about 8 km from the base of the ridge. From this view, the ridge's position belies the true bulk of this huge mountain massif that is so apparent on the King Trench route. An appreciation of size grows as climbers pull their sleds toward the base of the ridge.

Base camp is situated at 2400 m (7800 ft.) in the large bowl between the Hubsew Ridge and the bottom of the East Ridge. Alternatively, base camp can be placed out on the Hubbard Glacier on the north side of the ridge below McArthur Peak. Location of base camp should take into account avalanche runout zones.

From base camp, the ridge is gained by locating weaknesses such as snow couloirs that may approach 50° and involve an exposed bergschrund. Extra care should be taken around the low elevation rock bands especially on warm, sunny days, as rockfall has been a problem. Recent snow deposition can also make the couloirs susceptible to deadly avalanches. The 1957 first ascent gained the ridge from the north while a 1959 expedition added the currently more popular variation on the south side. Caches left at base camp should be well marked with extra long wands owing to significant snow accumulation. One party reported only .33 m (1 ft.) of their 5 m-long (16 ft.) wand remaining following a particularly snowy episode.

Camp 1 is shovelled out of the ridge crest below a rock band at 2700 m (8800 ft.). This rock band can be skirted en route to Camp 2 by a 50° ice gully on the

East Ridge of Mount Logan. Photo Chic Scott.

right (north) or climbed directly on its left side. Just before reaching Camp 2 at 3200 m (10,500 ft.) is a steep mixed section. There is much old, fixed line in various states of disrepair between Camp 1 and Camp 4 at 4100 m (13,500 ft.).

The route from Camp 2 to Camp 3 is highlighted by the first of two exciting knife-edge ridges. Ice screws come in handy for protection and most climbers will want to use two ice tools. Take care on the softer crest of the ridge, as the cornice has been known to calve off in its entirety, leaving the climber with a sudden unobstructed view of the Hubbard Glacier several hundred metres below. Camp 3 is usually placed immediately beyond this first knife-edge ridge at 3700 m (12,000 ft.).

Ascending the left (south) side of the ridge from Camp 3, sections of 50-60° ice are encountered as well as a small amount of rock. The final exhilarating knife-edge ridge is followed by crossing back and forth on less exposed terrain to Camp 4 at 4100 m (13,500 ft.).

The trip to Camp 5 begins with a pleasant 20-30° slope. Placing a few extra wands to better mark the trail between Camps 4 and 5 is a good idea. An icefall at 4400 m (14,500 ft.) is passed by traversing to the left (south) after weaving in and out of lower angle gullies and avoiding serac faces. A final 45° slope gives way to lower angle campsites at or above 4600 m (15,000 ft.). From this location, the technical difficulties on the East Ridge cease and the views of Mount MacCarthy and Mount Vancouver are stupendous.

A final Camp 6 is placed in the large bowl at 5200 m (17,000 ft.) below the prominent East Peak and may be located at the col in its upper end at about 5300 m (17,300 ft.).

On summit day, many parties elect to shorten the distance by opting for the East Peak. To gain the true summit, climb out of the bowl toward the East Peak and traverse across to the col between the East Peak and the main summit. Surmount the initial steep slope out of the col and follow the low angle summit ridge over stark, windswept terrain to the top. Weather permitting, the climber is rewarded with a stunning view of Mount Saint Elias to the southwest and the far off peaks in Alaska's Wrangell-Saint Elias National Park to the northwest. Parties report summit days commonly lasting 20+ hours.

Most parties return to the Hubbard Glacier for the return flight by downclimbing the East Ridge. It is also possible to traverse Mount Logan by descending the King Trench route, and this has been done, but this strategy presents problems in moving all gear and supplies up to the col between the East Peak and the main summit, and across the immense summit plateau. The difficulty in arranging a return charter flight back to civilization applies in any case.

[1] *50 Classic Climbs of North America,* Roper, Steve, and Carpé, Allen. Sierra Club Books, San Francisco, 1979, p. 37.
[2] "The Mount Logan Adventure," Allen Carpé, *American Alpine Journal*, 1933, p. 69-86.

Contacts

Tourism Yukon
P.O. Box 2703, Whitehorse, YT Y1A 2C6
Phone: 867-667-5340

Superintendent Kluane National Park
P.O. Box 5495, Haines Junction, YT Y0B 1L0
Phone: 867-634-2251

Icefield Ranges Expeditions
59 13th Avenue, Whitehorse, YT Y1A 4K6
Phone: 867-633-2018

Ultima Thule Outfitters
P.O. Box 109, Chitina, AK 99566
Phone: 907-258-0636

Gulf Air Taxi
P.O. Box 367, Yakutat, AK 99689
Phone: 907-784-3240

Additional Reading

"The Big One–A Guide to the Climbs of Mount Logan," *Canadian Alpine Journal*, Vol. 82, 1999. Compiled by Joe Josephson with maps by Gerald Holdsworth.
"The East Ridge of Mount Logan," Don Monk, *Canadian Alpine Journal*, Vol. 63, 1958, p. 17-23.
"A Logan Traverse," William Harrison, *American Alpine Journal*, Vol. 16, 1968, p. 46-50.

Mount Fairweather

British Columbia

4663 m (15,300 ft.)
Lat/long N58° 54' 25" W137° 31' 28"
UTM 355000m.E. 6532500m.N. (NAD 27)
Topo maps USGS Mount Fairweather (D-5, D6) Alaska
NTS 114 I/14 Mount Root

The mountaineer William S. Ladd, upon returning from a 1926 reconnaissance and attempted climb of the mountain, wrote the following: "Mount Fairweather...is a mountain of shining promise to those who would climb high. Its pyramidal central summit and broad shoulders, approached only by the steepest of great snow and ice aretes, give delight in a symmetrical grace and beauty that I know of no other great massif. Its fluted walls rise almost too steeply for the mountaineer on every side. The snow and ice hang as though glued upon them. Upon every line of approach that the eye follows in an effort to plan a route to the summit there is some obstacle demanding the best art of the mountaineer."[1]

Three to four hundred million years ago, shellfish, plankton, corals and other sea life lived and died in a warm, distant sea. In time, these creatures settled, solidified and became limestone, sandstone and siltstone. The fossils embedded in this rock were then carried northward on a long journey, moving at about 5 cm (2 in.) per year. They floated slowly on the earth's molten core, covering thousands of kilometres over a great span of time. When they finally collided with the North American plate, the heavier rocks were forced underneath, causing the plate to buckle and uplift. The original sedimentary layers were greatly distorted by heat and pressure and intruded with igneous matter, creating the varied and complex geology of today. These forces are still at work, continuing to shape and uplift this magnificent coastal range of mountains. Earthquakes occur regularly, and several major ones have been recorded. During the Lituya Bay earthquake of 1958, the plate to the west moved northwestward a full 6.5 m (21 ft.).

Tom and Dan Bennett on the Grand Plateau Glacier with the unclimbed Canadian face of Mount Fairweather in the clouds behind.

Uplifting of the Fairweather Range has set the stage for another sculpting process: glaciation. Moist air from the Pacific Ocean rises abruptly as it encounters the peaks. This causes the moisture to condense and fall as snow, accumulating up to 30 m (100 ft.) per year. The snow collects in mountain basins to great depths, then moves slowly downward as immense tidewater glaciers. Although some of these glaciers are retreating, most of the glaciers on the west side of Glacier Bay National Park are now either stable or are still advancing. All of these forces have conspired to produce one of the greatest and most majestic coastal mountain ranges in the world.

Mount Fairweather was reportedly first sighted by the captain of one of Vitus Bering's ships, the Saint Paul, in 1741, and was named by Captain James Cook during his voyage along the northwest coast of America in 1778. But Mount Fairweather was not seriously attempted until 1926 when Allen Carpé, William Ladd and Andy Taylor, fresh from their impressive first ascent of Mount Logan the year before, arrived at Lituya Bay on June 1 and began the arduous trck toward the west ridge of Mount Fairweather. After struggling for many days, the expedition reached an altitude of only 2800 m (9200 ft.), and retreated in the face of dwindling supplies. On another attempt, Bradford Washburn reached only 2040 m (6700 ft.) on the west ridge before being forced to retreat.

Carpé, Ladd and Taylor returned in 1931 for another attempt on Mount Fairweather, which by this time was known as the great unclimbed prize of North America. This time they were to succeed in what was acclaimed as the most demanding and technical route yet climbed on the continent. The towering Carpé Ridge of Mount Fairweather is still listed as one of the 50 classic climbs of North America. After that memorable ascent, Mount Fairweather was completely forgotten by climbers until 1958, over a quarter of a century later. In that year, British Columbia was celebrating its centennial, and an ascent of Mount Fairweather was chosen as a suitable feat to commemorate the event. After considerable fanfare and publicity, and after several weeks of work, the expedition succeeded in placing eight Canadians on the summit via a variation of Carpé's original route. The triumphant band returned to Lituya Bay and was picked up by the Royal Canadian Air Force on July 9 at 9:00 pm. Two hours after their departure, a gigantic earthquake rocked the region causing a wave of water to rise a full 550 m (1800 ft.) above sea level, scouring all timber and brush from the surrounding hills. This narrow miss, as well as continuing seismic activity, is a testament to the active forces still at work in the Fairweather Range.

In 1974 an expedition led by Walter Gove made a reconnaissance and attempt on the still unclimbed north side of Mount Fairweather. After landing on a small lake near the ocean, the party struggled onto the Upper Grand Plateau Glacier. They first considered the north buttress of Fairweather, but were discouraged by the huge ice cliffs and hanging glaciers that cap the whole north side of the mountain. The next day they set off for the saddle between the main peak and the much lower west peak, but were alarmed by the almost constant roar of avalanches sweeping across the route. They abandoned the climb.

In 1977 Walter Gove returned to the north side of Mount Fairweather together with Loren Adkins, George Fisher and Tom Distler. This time the

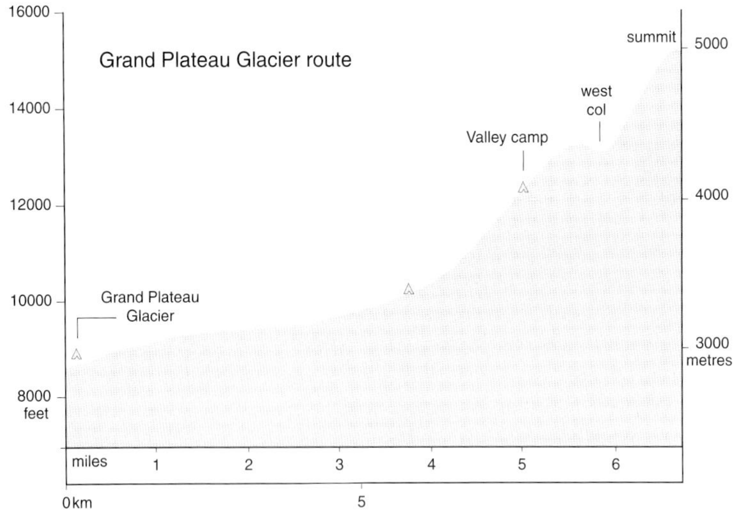

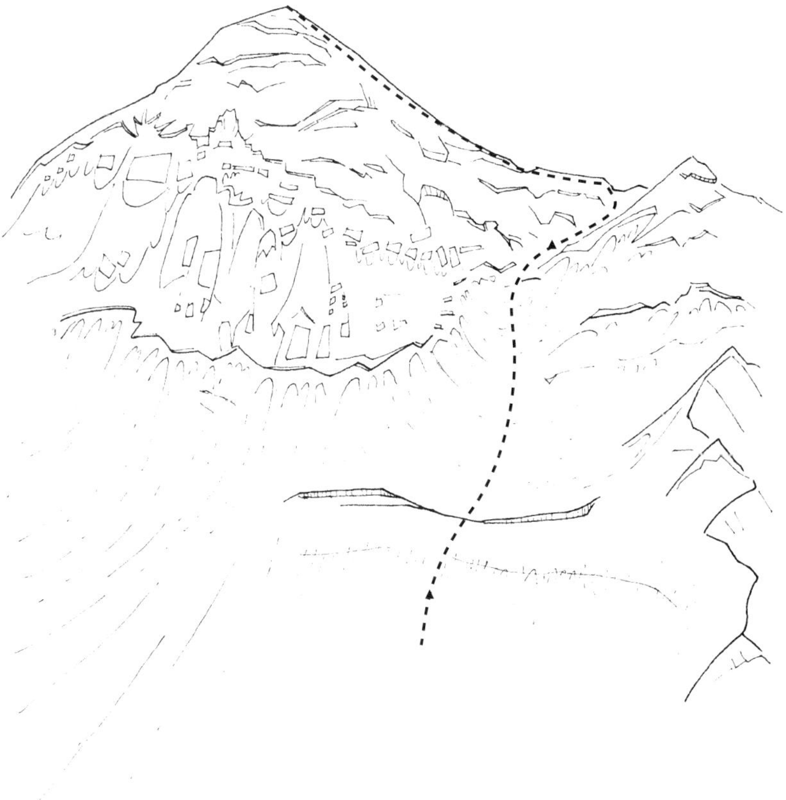

party avoided the risky valley by veering right onto the north ridge of the west peak. After traversing the west peak and descending to the col, they ascended the west ridge and completed the first ascent of Fairweather from the north. Today, most expeditions choose the technically easier, but more hazardous alternative of ascending the valley between Fairweather and its west peak, and accepting the risk of avalanche. This is now considered the easiest approach to the summit.

By 1979 Mount Fairweather had been climbed 10 times by six different routes. Each of these routes began at, or very near, the sea, as glacier landings and airdrops were forbidden within Glacier Bay National Park. This made Mount Fairweather an extremely difficult climb. An ascent "from sea to summit" became the standard practice for many years, and many climbers still disdain glacier landings in the region. But the recent allowance of glacier landings within the park has made the approach from the Upper Grand Plateau Glacier very attractive for those who want to achieve Mount Fairweather's summit. Even with the advent of glacier landings, Mount Fairweather's remoteness, lack of non-technical routes, and almost continual snowfall (reputed to exceed 30 m [100 ft.] per year) all contribute to keep it wilder and less visited than any other mountain of equal size in America.

Gulf Air Taxi, which flies out of Yakutat, Alaska, is the most commonly used air taxi service for the heart of the Fairweather Range. Yakutat is easily accessed, being serviced by scheduled commercial airlines twice each day, one northbound and one southbound. Gulf Air flies single engine Cessna 185s, which can carry two climbers plus gear per trip. They also rent a radiotelephone system that works very well for most of the area serviced. But be prepared: the notoriously foul weather in the range can cause long delays for both fly-in and fly-out. As has often been said about Mount McKinley in Alaska, and is perhaps even truer here, "This is waitin' country!" Gulf Air Taxi can land on the Grand Plateau Glacier at either 2700 or 3000 m (9000 or 10,000 ft.), and on the Fairweather Glacier at about 1600 m (5300 ft.). These sites are commonly used as base camps for attempts on Mount Fairweather.

Upper Grand Plateau Glacier to the West Ridge

This is the easiest and most used route on Mount Fairweather today. The 2700 m-high (9000 ft.) landing site on the Upper Grand Plateau Glacier is probably the more sensible choice to allow for better acclimatization. This landing site is only about 8 km (5 mi.) north-northwest of Mount Fairweather.

The approach to the mountain up the gradually ascending Grand Plateau Glacier is straightforward, and one can camp almost anywhere. Crevasse danger here is minimal, but parties should travel roped as a precaution. There are two possible routes from the glacier to the summit, and both can be used. The first ascent party, alarmed by the almost constant roar of avalanches into the valley between Fairweather and its west peak, chose to ascend the north ridge of the west peak, then descend to the col. More recent expeditions have chosen to ascend the valley directly to the col and move quickly through the avalanche hazard. This latter route is easier, but is also more dangerous. This is the route described here in detail.

Enter the valley between Fairweather and its west peak at about 3500 m (11,500 ft.). The most serious avalanche danger extends a few hundred metres, from about 3500 m (11,500 ft.) to 3660 m (12,000 ft.), owing to hanging glaciers on both Mount Fairweather and its west peak. The most dangerous ground is littered with avalanche debris. Avalanches can release any time of day here, and you would be well advised to locate campsites either below or above this hazard. A summit day starting below the valley would be very long and hard indeed, and a higher camp is strongly recommended. In any case, move as quickly as possible through the avalanche debris. Once above 3660 m (12,000 ft.), the avalanche danger is minimal.

From a campsite high in the valley, move directly toward the col between Mount Fairweather and its west peak. Crevasse hazard is more serious toward the upper end of the valley. The headwall to the col is moderately steep, and is typically soft snow. This headwall is easier on the right. Once the col is gained, the snow will become ice, and crampons can be used for the assault on the final summit ridge.

Walk over the small hill in the centre of the col and directly ascend the moderate, 600 m-long (2000 ft.) west ridge of Mount Fairweather. Conditions on the ridge will vary from occasional deep powder to hard wind-driven ice. Ice mushrooms are common high on the ridge. An occasional steep step will be encountered, as well as a few large crevasses, but in most years the technical difficulties presented by the ridge will not be great. As the weather of the region is highly unpredictable, and good conditions seldom last long, parties should carefully mark the ascent route with wands all the way to the summit. From a camp at 3660 m (12,000 ft.), the summit is only about 2.5 km (1.5 mi.) distant, but the climb on summit day can be expected to take 12 to 16 hours owing to deep snow and difficult weather conditions.

From the summit good weather will provide the climber with a spectacular view, as Fairweather rises high above its neighbouring peaks. A unique combination of peaks, glaciers and ocean is a special attraction of the Fairweather Range.

Return to the col, the valley and the Grand Plateau Glacier by the same route in reverse.

Carpé Ridge

The Carpé Ridge, although less commonly climbed than the West Ridge, is still chosen by about one out of four expeditions today. At the time of its first ascent in 1931, the towering Carpé Ridge was considered a very difficult and technical ascent. Modern climbers no longer consider the technical difficulties severe, but neither do they take them lightly. The route is not one to stumble carelessly down in the dark. With the exception of a few hundred metres on the shoulder, the angle is unrelenting and any fall on ice would be difficult to self-arrest.

Viewed from the south and west, the summit of Mount Fairweather forms a pyramid. The South Ridge forms a distinctive shoulder of the mountain. Proceeding downwards, this ridge branches into two, forming a wishbone. The left, or southwest branch, is the Carpé Ridge.

Looking up the mountain from the Fairweather Glacier near the base of the route at 1400 m (4600 ft.), one sees an icefall just left of the ridge. The ridge itself is a lumpy series of rock piles, with steep rock on the left and snowfields on the right. The first problem is to gain access to the snowfields just to the right of the ridge proper while coping with the icefall and rock cliffs as little as possible. The best strategy is probably to skirt the icefall in the snowy right margin and find a reasonable access right through the rock bands. This access is best accomplished after about 200 m (700 ft.) of elevation gain, where a horizontal traverse under the first ridge pillar allows access to the snowfields on the right of the ridge. Depending on the condition of the icefall along the right margin of the rock, expect some messy and potentially tricky problems when surmounting ice blocks or vertical snow mushrooms.

The traverse is on approximately 40° snow/ice. As soon as you are right of the ridgeline, head up through the snowfield. Depending on the route chosen, one or two rock bands at about 2100 m (7000 ft.) will have to be ascended before gaining the upper snowfield. The angle in this fourth-class rock band is not severe, perhaps 50°. If you are planning on ascending this section more than once to stock a high camp, you might want to fix 100 m (330 ft.) of 7 or 8 mm-thick rope here (but be sure to retrieve the rope as you depart the mountain!). Descent through the rock bands with heavy packs would probably best be accomplished on rappel.

After passing the band the angle eases a bit as you ascend the snowfields right of the pillared ridge. As the elevation increases, expect more ice and less snow. With sections of ice climbing approaching 45° here, many parties will want to put in a few ice screws. Near the top of the pillared ridge, at about 3000 m (9700 ft.), one will find some fairly level spots to place a camp. It is best to stop shy of the top of the lower ridge, however, so as to have a less exposed campsite. These are really the first comfortably level spots since leaving the Fairweather Glacier. The trek to this point is a very long, but doable one-day climb with packs. The views from here across the glacier to Mounts Lituya and Sabine are spectacular. The ridges on those peaks are inviting as secondary objectives, assuming the ascent of Fairweather goes well.

It makes sense to make a second trip from base camp to stock this high camp. Otherwise, the ascent to the summit would have to be accomplished with minimal chance to acclimatize. You should be prepared to sit out a coastal storm, but periods of good weather are also possible during the summer.

The summit can be reached in one hard push from high camp. This makes for another long day, with 1700 m (5500 ft.) of elevation gain. But with the lengthy daylight of the near Arctic summer, this should not be a problem for an energetic party.

At the top of the pillared ridge are broad open slopes, occasionally steepening to 50°. At about 3500 m (11,500 ft.) there is a section of knife-edge ridge, then a broad, nearly level shoulder as you approach the summit pyramid. Deep snow can slow progress here. A high camp could be established on this shoulder at 4100 m (13,500 ft.), but given good weather and a willingness to descend in the evening twilight, the tendency is to push on to the summit.

The last technical obstacle on the route is the "ice nose" part way up the summit pyramid. The configuration of the ice will vary from year to year, but expect one-and-a-half pitches of ice at 50-60°. A few screws and a second ice tool are advisable here as the difficulties occur at nearly 4600 m (15,000 ft.) and toward the end of a very long day of climbing. A snow anchor may be needed for a descent on rappel here. A few wands might be a good idea, as well, to be sure of finding the spot in a whiteout.

Return to the Fairweather Glacier by the ascent route, making sure to retrieve any wands and fixed rope left during the ascent.

[1] "The Fairweather Mountains," William S. Ladd, *American Alpine Journal*, Vol. 1, 1929.

Contacts

Yakutat District Warden, Glacier Bay National Park
P.O. Box 137, Yakutat, AK 99689
Phone: Yakutat District Warden 907-784-3295, Glacier Bay 907-697-2230

Gulf Air Taxi, Inc.
P.O. Box 367, Yakutat, AK 99689
Phone: 907-784-3240

Additional Reading

"The Conquest of Mount Fairweather," Allen Carpé and Terris Moore, *Alpine Journal,* Nov. 1931, Vol. 43, p. 221.

"The West Ridge of Mt. Fairweather," Walter Gove and Loren Adkins, *American Alpine Journal,* 1969, p. 304-307.

"Mount Watson and the Grand Plateau Glacier," Walter Gove and Donald Lisich, *American Alpine Journal,*1974, p. 43-46.

"Mount Fairweather: America's Little-Known Giant," Peter Metcalf, *Summit,* April-May 1977, p. 3-9.

"The Grand Plateau Glacier Revisited," Walter Gove, *American Alpine Journal,* 1978, p. 397-402.

"Mount Fairweather, The First Ten Ascents," Bradford Washburn, *American Alpine Journal,* 1981, p. 29-353.

Mount Columbia

Alberta

3747 m (12,294 ft.)
Lat/long N52° 08' 52" W117° 26' 23"
UTM 469850m.E. 5777300m.N. (NAD 27)
Topo map 83 C/3 Columbia Icefield

The Canadian Rockies extend nearly 3000 km (1900 mi.) from Montana to Alaska. These magnificant mountains, although lower in elevation than the Rockies in the United States, are generally more spectacular and alpine-like owing to extensive glaciation. The spine of the Rockies forms the Continental Divide that separates Alberta from British Columbia in Banff and Jasper national parks. The mountains here are composed largely of limestone, sandstone and shale laid down during the Precambrian and Cretaceous periods. About 70 million years ago, forces resulted in faulting, folding and uplifting these rock layers to produce the magnificent mountain ranges of today.

The highest point in the Canadian Rockies is the dramatic and difficult Mount Robson at 3954 m (12,972 ft.). But Mount Robson is not a provincial highpoint as it lies wholly within British Columbia, and several mountains in the Coast Range of that province exceed its height. The highest point in Alberta is the beautiful Mount Columbia, 3747 m (12,294 ft.), near the southern edge of Jasper National Park.

Mount Columbia juts out of the northern edge of the massive Columbia Icefield, the largest icefield in the Rocky Mountains. The Columbia Icefield straddles 325 sq. km (125 sq. mi.) of the Great Divide that separates Alberta from British Columbia. This icefield basin, together with the high surrounding peaks, cause moisture-laden winds blowing eastward from the Pacific to rise abruptly, resulting in a massive amount of precipitation in the form of rain or snow. Snowfall on the Columbia Icefield is estimated at a dramatic 9 m (30 ft.) per year. Snow and ice have accumulated to depths of greater than 300 m (1000 ft.), and no less than six major glaciers flow outward from the icefield. The southern and eastern slopes of Mount Columbia itself are completely buried in glacial ice.

Approaching the east face of Mount Columbia. The prominent ridge in the centre is the usual ascent route.

Mount Columbia was named by Norman Collie, who was the first to view the Columbia Icefield and surrounding peaks from the summit of Mount Athabasca in 1898. This exploration attracted the attention of James Outram, who came to the Canadian Rockies in 1900 to recover his health after suffering a nervous breakdown. Outram was inspired to climb the peaks, and stunned the North American mountaineering community in 1902 by climbing 10 peaks that were each over 3050 m (10,000 ft.). One of the most striking achievements of Outram, together with the Swiss guide Christian Kaufmann, was the first ascent of Mount Columbia in July 1902. The two climbers pioneered the east face route, which is still the standard route on the mountain. The vast majority of climbers, more than 90 percent, still ascend Mount Columbia by its east face. The next most frequented route, the North Ridge route, is much more difficult and is, by comparison, very seldom climbed.

The usual approach to the mountain is via the Athabasca Glacier from Alberta Highway 93, known as the Icefields Parkway, about 100 km (60 mi.) south of Jasper, Alberta. This is the route described below. About 20 per cent of those who climb Mount Columbia approach via the Saskatchewan Glacier, which is much longer, but is considered by some to be a safer route. Although the east face of Mount Columbia is not regarded as a technically difficult climb, adverse snow and weather conditions can make it a challenging and tiring climb any time of year. The weather on the Columbia Icefield is highly unpredictable, and good conditions seldom last long.

The area near the toe of the Athabasca Glacier is a popular tourist stop, and during the summer the scene is a bustle of activity. The Columbia Icefield Chalet, located here, was built by Brewster Transport in 1939, and is still available for lodging. A campground is located just 3 km (2 mi.) farther south. The area near the chalet also has a snack building, a visitor centre and warden office, and several service buildings. It is necessary to register all climbs and overnight hikes at the warden office. The itinerary of the trip must be carefully considered, as failure to return at the appointed hour will launch a rescue effort.

A single road branches south from the Icefields Parkway at an elevation of 1987 m (6518 ft.). A right fork leads tourists to the toe of the Athabasca Glacier, while the left fork is used by Brewster Transport to access the upper portions of the glacier. The left fork of the road is restricted, and is blocked by a gate that is closed during the day, but open at night. Beyond this gate, about 1 km (0.6 mi.) from Highway 93, is the climbers' parking lot. One can drive directly to this parking lot at night or early in the morning, but during the day it is necessary to wait for a Brewster Transport bus to open the gate, then follow it through. The climbers' parking lot, at an elevation of about 2040 m (6700 ft.), is the farthest private cars can proceed, as the road is blocked by a second gate just beyond this parking lot.

From the climbers' parking lot, pack about 1 km (0.6 mi.) up to the Brewster Transport staging area, where tourists switch from highway buses to snowcoaches. Thousands of visitors each year ride the Brewster Transport snowcoaches down the steep lateral moraine and onto the surface of the Athabasca Glacier. The snowcoaches carry passengers another 2 km (1.2 mi.) to an altitude of about 2260 m (7400 ft.) on the flat, lower surface of the glacier. Pack to the parking lot at the end of the snowcoach road, and rope-up before walking beyond the parking lot.

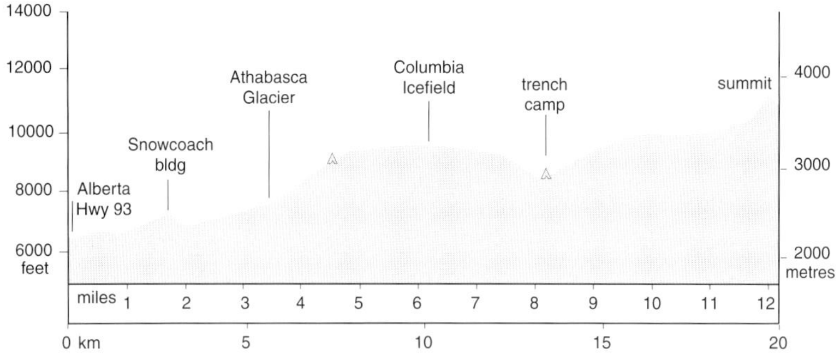

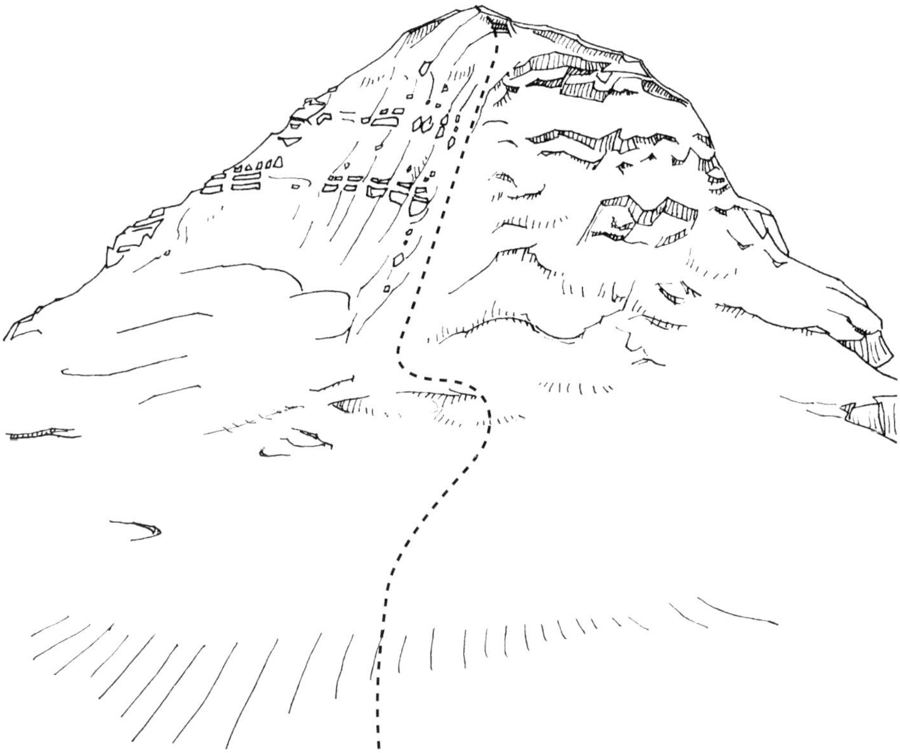

The Athabasca Glacier has three major icefalls. The lower two icefalls are heavily crevassed and must be passed on either the right or the left. Both sides are threatened by ice and rock fall, and should be passed as quickly as possible. The right side is easier and is the recommended route. An easy ramp leads up the centre of the third icefall to the Columbia Icefield.

Once on the icefield, head directly for a large trench about 7 km (4.4 mi.) east of Mount Columbia. It may be useful to follow a compass bearing of 210° (magnetic declination is 22° 10') across the icefield, as bad weather conditions are not unusual. Snowshoes or skis should be taken to cope with soft snow conditions. Once well away from the Athabasca Glacier there is minimal crevasse danger until the steeper sides of the trench are approached. Make camp in or near the trench, at an elevation of 2710 m (8900 ft.). This is a long first day, gaining 880 m (2900 ft.) in elevation, then descending 210 m (700 ft.) to the bottom of the trench over a total distance of about 13 km (8 mi.).

The Columbia Icefield is quite flat, and it is possible to glacier-land with fixed-wing aircraft, either east or west of the trench. But this only eliminates a single day of effort, and hardly seems worth the trouble and expense.

From a camp in the trench, proceed west toward Mount Columbia, easily bypassing crevasses on the side of the trench. Continue about 4 km (2.5 mi.) west to the base of the summit pyramid.

The east face of Mount Columbia, called the southeast face by the first ascent party, is about 610 m (2000 ft.) high, and angles about 45° at its steepest section. This face is usually climbed on its left (south) side, but is sometimes climbed on the right. If the snow is soft and unconsolidated, it may be prone to avalanche. The difficulty of the climb will vary according to time of year and weather conditions, but normally the east face can be climbed without difficulty.

Once the top of the east face is reached, scramble northwest down a couple of metres, then up to the true summit, which is only slightly higher. This summit day gains 1040 m (3400 ft.) over a total distance of almost 7 km (4.4. mi.).

To return to trench camp, and the Athabasca Glacier, follow the same route in reverse.

Contacts

British Columbia Provincial Parks
800 Johnson Street, 2nd Floor, Victoria, BC V8V 1X4
Phone: 250-387-5002 or 1-800-663-6000

Alberta Economic Development and Tourism
P.O. Box 2500, Edmonton, AB T5J 2Z4
Phone: 780-292-4401 or 1-800-661-8888

Superintendent, Banff National Park
P.O. Box 900, Banff, AB TOL OCO
Phone: 403-762-1550, Warden's Office: 403-762-1470

Superintendent, Jasper National Park
P.O. Box 10, Jasper, AB TOE 1EO
Phone: 780-852-6161, Icefield Office: 780-852-5383

Guide book
Selected Alpine Climbs in the Canadian Rockies by Sean Dougherty, Rocky Mountain Books, Calgary, revised ed., 1996.

Mount Nirvana

Northwest Territories

2773 m (9097 ft.)
Lat/long N61° 52' 31" W127° 40' 38"
UTM 569450m.E. 6860750m.N. (NAD 27)
Topo maps 95 E/13 Mount Sidney Dobson
and 95 E/14 Hole in the Wall Lake

A spectacularly wild and little-known series of mountain ranges lies near the Yukon border in the southwest corner of the Northwest Territories. These mountain ranges consist mostly of sedimentary peaks from the Paleozoic era. During the Cretaceous period, a massive intrusion forced its way up through the overlying sediments, and was later exposed and shaped by powerful rivers and glaciers. The result was one of the most striking mountain ranges to be found in North America, the MacKenzie Mountains. In a sub-range of the MacKenzies, known as the Logan Mountains, towering domes and pinnacles rise majestically 1500 m (5000 ft.) above the surrounding plains. Concealed deep within the Southern Logan Mountains, in a cluster of dramatic spires known as the Ragged Range, is Mount Nirvana, the highest mountain in the Northwest Territories.

Mount Nirvana remains a mystery, seldom visited and practically unknown. Nearly every atlas and reference publication lists Mount Sir James McBrian as the highest point of the Northwest Territories. Mount Sir James McBrian is one of a remarkable group of spires known collectively as "The Cirque of the Unclimbables." Here, in a place that has become fabled in the world of technical rock climbing, granite spires soar 670 m (2200 ft.) above Fairy Meadow. The Lotus Flower Tower is an especially imposing spire with several perfectly formed vertical cracks, each an inch or two wide, which rise straight to the summit. It is a sight to be seen nowhere else. But 30 km (19 mi.) farther south in the Ragged Range of the Logan Mountains is another group of jagged peaks, one of which rises 14 m (46 ft.) higher than Mount Sir James McBrian. The peak is not officially named and its elevation is not reported on the 1:50,000 map Mount Sidney Dobson. On that map, the true significance of Nirvana is obscured by the summit's sharpness, which does not allow plotting of all of its contour lines. On the 1:250,000 map Flat River, only an insignificant elevation mark betrays its existence.

But climbers know Mount Nirvana. John Milton led the first serious climbing expedition into the region in 1960. Milton and Ed Arnold landed at Hole-in-the-Wall Lake, and after conducting ecological research and exploration of the valley they decided to make their way west over the tangle of passes and peaks in an effort to reach the highest summits. Arnold fell and was injured while attempting to cross the second wall of peaks that blocked their way, but Milton continued on to make the first ascent of Mount Savage. From the summit of Mount Savage, Milton described a magnificent peak to the west. "...flanked by a complex series of glaciers, the summit of Mount Nahanni reared its granite head into the gathering stormclouds."[1] The dramatic mountain that Milton called "Mount Nahanni" would later be named "Mount Nirvana."

That same year, from the summits of the Cirque of the Unclimbables, Bill Buckingham's eyes lingered longingly on a fine group of peaks far to the south. After pouring over maps and the little information available, Buckingham and Lew Surdam landed at Lonely Lake in Hole-in-the-Wall Valley in July 1965. They reported a difficult and gruelling journey to finally reach a position just south of Mount Nirvana. Climbing to the western end of the Gargoyle Ridge, they viewed the stupendous southern walls and turrets of Nirvana. They concluded that any route from the south or east would be more of an undertaking than they were prepared for, and decided to seek a route from the north. They struggled to circle the mountain on the west, and finally entered the great sanctuary north of Nirvana. From their camp in this fantastic cirque, they managed to climb the glacier, cross the bergschrund, and ascend the northwest ridge to the summit. Their descent was made in total darkness, and they finally crawled into their sleeping bags in the steely light of dawn the next morning. This courageous and determined first ascent of Mount Nirvana would not be repeated for another 10 years.

In 1975, Alan Embick, Al Long and Tod Thompson avoided the exhausting approach by simply landing a helicopter in the sanctuary on the north side of Mount Nirvana. From here the three completed several first ascents of the enormous rock towers surrounding them. They also completed the second ascent of Nirvana via a new route on the north face. Although the mountains surrounding Hole-in-the-Wall Valley saw some climbing activity in the ensuing years, Nirvana was apparently not climbed by this or any other route until 1996.

The most difficult problem in any assault on Mount Nirvana is the approach. Of course, climbers could avoid the question by simply hiring a helicopter to deposit them at the base of the mountain. But aside from being expensive, this seems a little like cheating, as the approach to the mountain is an integral part of the Nirvana experience. None of the air charter services in the area is equipped to land on glaciers, and it has not been established that such a landing would even be possible on the small glaciers nearby. Likewise, the nearest lakes large enough to permit a landing by floatplane are several kilometres away, over difficult terrain.

The only reasonable way to approach the north face on Mount Nirvana is by landing at Rabbitkettle Lake in Nahanni National Park. A landing at Rabbitkettle Lake can also be used to access the east face. But travel up the Rabbitkettle River is very unpleasant indeed. Travel below 1500 m (5000 ft.) elevation in the Southern Logan Mountains is characterized by dense brush, heavy mats of reindeer moss, extensive swamps and hordes of voracious mosquitoes. Another obvious possibility is to land at one of the lakes in Hole-in-the-Wall Valley, as did John Milton and Bill Buckingham, and journey over two high mountain barriers to reach the east face of Nirvana. Most of this route is at elevations above 1500 m (5000 ft.) where the terrain may be technically difficult, but is distinctly more pleasurable. Unfortunately, the authorities at Nahanni National Park will not permit a landing on either Hole-in-the-Wall Lake or Lonely Lake. Unless this policy changes, the approach to Mount Nirvana will remain a very troublesome problem.

The weather in the Southern Logan Mountains is usually unsettled. Rain and drizzle can set in at any time, and may last for days. Mountain goats, mountain sheep and elk are all common, and precautions must be taken against contact with both black bears and grizzly bears.

Fixed-wing aircraft can be chartered from Watson Lake, Fort Liard, Fort Nelson or Fort Simpson. These include Deh Cho Air, Liard Air, Simpson Air, Wolverine Air, Blackstone Aviation and Watson Lake Air.

Rabbitkettle River

Rabbitkettle Lake is a 2 km-long (1.25 mi.) lake located near the mouth of the Rabbitkettle River and about .5 km (.3 mi.) from the Nahanni River. It is a common staging point for canoe trips on the Nahanni River, and Nahanni National Park maintains a backcountry campground at the south end of the lake. There is also a dock and a small cabin where one or two park wardens are stationed during the summer.

From the lake, a well-maintained trail leads south across Hot Springs Valley to the Rabbitkettle River. The river is swift and deep at this point, but a hand-operated ferry can be used to cross to the south bank. Wardens schedule ferry crossings to conduct tours of the Rabbitkettle Hot Springs on the far side. From the hot springs, the only trails leading upriver are scattered game trails.

The first 8 km (5 mi.) up the Rabbitkettle River are extremely difficult. There are no game trails to follow here. Trying to follow a straight line means encountering dense brush, blowdowns and swamps. Following the riverbank gives an occasional respite in the form of easy gravel bars, but the total distance travelled is much longer as the river meanders. In either case, Nightwind Creek must be crossed about 5 km (3 mi.) up the river. Nightwind Creek here is swift and wide, and may be especially hazardous in early summer.

The sanctuary on the north side of Mount Nirvana. Nirvana is the rounded peak near the centre.

After about 8 km (5 mi.) up the river the valley narrows. Here game trails become more common and make the travel somewhat easier. But the game trails are capricious, frequently disappearing and reappearing, and require considerable effort to follow. This section continues along the Rabbitkettle River for about 12 km (7.5 mi.) until the creek is reached, which drains the east side of Mount Nirvana. At this point the routes to the east and north faces diverge.

Theoretically, it would be possible to follow this stream up to the east face of Nirvana. However, no one has reported taking this approach, and it would surely not be an easy task. This route can be expected to have very dense brush, boulder fields and thick mats of reindeer moss. The climb up the east face of Mount Nirvana is described under the Hole-in-the-Wall Valley route.

From this stream, the next 8 km (5 mi.) up the Rabbitkettle River are much worse than the previous terrain. Boulder fields become increasingly difficult, and game trails disappear.

The second major stream from the south leads directly up to the great sanctuary north of Mount Nirvana. But just when it seems that the travel could not be any more difficult, it gets much worse. The last 6 km (3.75 mi.) up to the sanctuary can be expected to take several hours. Finally a waterfall appears in the distance at about 1480 m (4900 ft.). Above this waterfall, brush and talus suddenly give way to glorious meadows surrounded by towering granite spires. These meadows provide a convenient location for a summit camp.

Summit day from a camp in the meadows will be very long. Above the meadows, a pair of steep icefalls cascade down from either side of a prow-like nunatak. The icefall on the left is the preferred route, and is easiest immediately adjacent to the nunatak. At the top of the nunatak, the north face of Mount Nirvana looms above. The first challenge is to cross the bergschrund, the crack that separates the moving glacier from the stationary wall of granite. The far wall of the bergschrund is several metres high, and is overhanging in places. The 'schrund may be spanned by a snowbridge on the right, which is the route taken by the first ascent party. The snow slope above the snowbridge may be unstable, depending on conditions. If the snowbridge is present, work up and slightly left to gain the northwest ridge. The climbing here is mixed between rock and snow, and holds are frequently wet and loose. At times it will be possible to follow the ridge crest. At other times it will be necessary to traverse out onto the north face to avoid a tower or steep step. The final wall below the summit must be passed on the left. Buckingham reported passing behind an awkward slippery chockstone and a final strenuous overhanging crack leading to the summit.

Alan Embick crossed the bergschrund on the left of the face and climbed diagonally up to the right to reach the summit. This route may be the easier of the two if conditions are favourable to cross the 'schrund. But no one can objectively compare the two routes as they have each been climbed only once.

The face may be descended by rappelling directly down, but difficulty may be encountered finding secure rappel anchors. The route of ascent may also be descended, but this will involve some downclimbing because of the diagonal nature of the route.

After climbing Mount Nirvana, retrace the route back to the Rabbitkettle River and Rabbitkettle Lake. The hardships and effort of the return journey should not be underestimated, particularly after the strenuous approach and summit climb.

Hole-in-the-Wall Valley

Hole-in-the-Wall Valley is a secluded valley in the southern tip of Nahanni National Park. There are two lakes in the valley suitable for landing by floatplanes. The first, and largest, lake in the chain is Hole-in-the-Wall Lake, at an elevation of about 1170 m (3800 ft.). The second lake in the valley is Lonely Lake, about 6 km (3.75 mi.) farther west, at an elevation of about 1350 m (4400 ft.). Unfortunately, Nahanni National Park authorities do not permit a landing at either of these lakes. Park officials have recommended landing just outside the park boundary at a small lake 5 km (3 mi.) southeast of Hole-in-the-Wall Lake. But this lake is very small, and most charter pilots will not attempt a landing. This approach is therefore very problematic.

If Hole-in-the-Wall Valley can be accessed, continue west up the valley through low brush about 3 km (2 mi.) beyond Lonely Lake to Beaver Lake, the last in a series of lakes in the valley. Beaver Lake, at about 1480 m (4900

The east face of Mount Nirvana. Photo Tony Daffern.

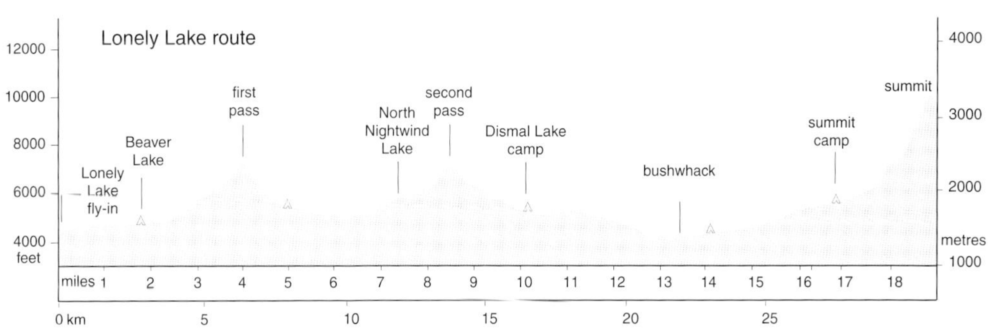
Lonely Lake route
12000
10000
8000
6000
4000
feet
4000
3000
2000
1000
metres
Lonely Lake fly-in
Beaver Lake
first pass
North Nightwind Lake
second pass
Dismal Lake camp
bushwhack
summit camp
summit
miles 1 2 3 4 5 6 7 8 9 10 11 12 13 14 15 16 17 18
0 km 5 10 15 20 25

ft.), roughly separates the difficult terrain of the lower elevations from the more open easy ground of the higher elevations.

From Beaver Lake, climb west through alpine meadows to a pass (GR 798512) at about 2150 m (7100 ft.). This pass is steep, especially on the west side, but is not technical and is easily climbed. From the pass, descend northwest down the valley ahead toward Nightwind Creek. The meadows near Nightwind Creek make a good campsite.

The next barrier of mountains is very difficult, and is the crux of this approach route. The vertical walls and towers above South Nightwind Lake are very technical, and not at all suitable for travel with heavy packs. The next pass to the north is also very technical, particularly on the west, and may also be difficult with full packs. But it may be possible to cross this pass by rappelling down the west side. The next pass (GR 773572), northwest of North Nightwind Lake, is easily crossed to a small glacier on the far side. This pass, at an elevation of about 2220 m (7300 ft.) provides an easy passage west, but also adds about 7 km (4.4 mi.) to the approach route. This pass was the one used by John Milton in 1960, and by the Bennett party in 1996.

If this easier pass is taken, descend the glacier into a dismal, narrow valley choked with boulder fields. Continue north down this valley, finally descending to the creek that drains the east face of Mount Nirvana. Unfortunately, this means descending to an elevation of about 1200 m (3900 ft.), into the brush and mosquitoes of the lower elevations. Once down to the main valley, ascend the stream about 4 km (2.5 mi.) to the valley junction immediately east of Nirvana. The terrain up the valley is difficult. Finally, climb grassy slopes to about 1700 m (5600 ft.), and make a summit camp in the meadows just east of Nirvana.

From summit camp, ascend the valley to the right side of the glacier that descends from Mount Nirvana. Rope up before venturing onto the glacier, which is heavily crevassed. Continue west on the flat glacier to the bergschrund, the crack that separates the moving glacier from the rock. This bergschrund is much smaller than the one on the north face and is easily crossed. Cross the 'schrund and ascend a broken band of rock to a large snowfield at the base of the face. The snowfield is about 50°, and is easily climbed to a broken series of rocks leading to the steepest portion of the face, a 150 m-high (492 ft.) band of granite. This rock band is the crux of the route. The rock band is climbed by angling slightly left for several rope lengths toward the left end of a broad snow ledge. The rock in the band is generally sound, but may be wet and slippery. The difficulty of the climbing is up to about 5.7 YDS.

Once the snow ledge is reached, traverse right on the ledge about 50 m (160 ft.). From here, climb up and left on narrow ledges, aiming for a large detached flake on the skyline. Climb over the detached flake and ascend a final strenuous chock-filled chimney to the south ridge of Nirvana. Once on the south ridge, ascend an exposed knife-edge snow arête and continue up the south ridge toward the summit. A few easy steps lead to the cairn built just below the summit by Bill Buckingham in 1965.

The face may be descended by rappelling down from the south ridge.

Return to Hole-in-the-Wall Valley by retracing the same route in reverse. Alternatively, the return route may be shortened by climbing over Nightwind Peak, and rappelling down the vertical cliffs above South Nightwind Lake. This is a difficult 150 m-long (490 ft.) rappel. The return to Hole-in-the-Wall Valley will take at least three days, even with the shortcut over South Nightwind Lake.

[1] "Southern Logan Mountains Expedition," John Milton, *Canadian Alpine Journal*, 1962, p. 36-48.

Contacts

Economic Development and Tourism
Government of the Northwest Territories
P.O. Box 1320, Yellowknife, NWT X1A 2L9
Phone: 1-800-661-0788

Nahanni National Park Reserve
P.O. Box 346, Fort Simpson, NWT X0E 0N0
Phone: 867-695-3151 fax: 867-695-2446

Deh Cho Air, Ltd.
Box 78, Fort Liard, NWT X0G 0A0
Phone: 867-770-4103 fax: 867-770-4102

Liard Tours, Ltd.
P.O. Box 3140, Fort Nelson, BC V0C 1R0
Phone: 250-774-2909

Simpson Air, Ltd.
P.O. Box 260, Fort Simpson, NWT X0E 0N0
Phone: 867-695-2505

Wolverine Air, Ltd.
Box 316, Fort Simpson, NWT X0E 0N0
Phone: 867-695-2263

Additional Reading

"Southern Logan Mountains Expedition," John Milton, *Canadian Alpine Journal,* 1962, p. 36-48.
"Logan Mountains, 1965," William J. Buckingham, *American Alpine Journal,* 1966, p. 33-37.
"Southern Logan Mountains, NWT," Peter Rowat, *Canadian Alpine Journal,* 1969, p. 1-4.
"Logan Mountains," Andrew Embick, *American Alpine Journal,* 1976, p. 320-325.

Barbeau Peak

Nunavut

2670 m (8769 ft.)
Lat/long N75° 00' 43" W81° 54' 51"
UTM 499814m.E. 9095125m.N. (NAD 27)
Topo map 340D Tanquary Fiord (1:250, 000)

"During the brief arctic summer on Ellesmere Island, the sun remains high in the sky bathing the land in continuous daylight. There is no darkness to mark the passage of time telling you when to sleep and when to wake. There are no trees to remind you of lands further south. The scale of the land is both immense and intimate at the same time. Intricate patterns of rock, frost-cracked ground, willows and wildflowers at your feet extend out from where you stand into endless vistas in the clear, dry air. Glaciers on a mountainside 15 km away seem to be details in a landscape within reach.

"Animals in the park appear innocent in their lack of fear of people. Long-tailed jaegers may hover in front of you while caribou may approach you closely, each curious of your presence.

"The signs of men and women that came before you are still clearly evident even though some are 4,000 years old. A stone fox trap, a tent ring (a circle of boulders marking a campsite), and scattered remains of the equipment of North Pole exploration parties all speak of the courage and the adventurous spirit of those who first came to this solitude at the top of the world.

"They are all reminders that, regardless of where you have come from, you are a long way from home."

The above lines from an Quttinirtaaq (Ellesmere Island) National Park brochure best describe the dramatic setting surrounding Barbeau Peak, the highpoint of Nunavut.

High above the icecap of Ellesmere Island, the Innuitian Mountains stand like icy watchtowers. These lonely mountains are folded sedimentary rocks uplifted during the Mesozoic era. They resemble the Appalachian Mountains in composition, but as they are much younger, have not yet

The author sled hauling across the Ellesmere Icecap. Barbeau Peak is above his left shoulder. Photo Tony Daffern.

eroded much. The slopes of the Innuitian Mountains are today buried up to 900 m (3000 ft.) deep in glacial ice, remains of the last great continental glacier that covered North America 10,000 years ago. The highest mountains are west of Lake Hazen in a range that extends northeast to southwest for about 25 km (15.5 mi.). The highest of these is a slender summit known as Barbeau Peak.

The first explorer to see this range of mountains was Adolphus A. Greely from Lake Hazen during his western journey of 1882. His notes mention a very high peak that he named Mount Whisler, but the foothills surrounding Lake Hazen hid the highest summit. The few expeditions, notably those of Robert E. Peary that passed through the Lake Hazen Valley over the next 50 years, were concerned only with hunting and a route north toward the North Pole. In 1935, an expedition led by A. W. Moore of Oxford University climbed and named Mount Oxford. From its summit, Moore surmised that the highest peaks lay far to the northwest in mountains that he named the British Empire Range. But 22 years later, an expedition led by G. Hattersley-Smith determined the highest peak of the British Empire Range to be about 2300 m (7,500 ft.). More than 300 m (1000 ft.) higher, however, was the flat-topped summit of Mount Whisler and the ridge that stretched beyond it toward the southwest.

In the spring of 1962, Hattersley-Smith accompanied Paul Atkinson on an altimetric survey of the highest peaks on northern Ellesmere Island. The pilot, flying a single-engine Otter aircraft, skimmed past the peaks at summit level while Atkinson recorded their heights. The results showed a sharp peak about 15 km (9 mi.) southwest of Mount Whisler to be the highest. This was later named "Barbeau Peak" in honour of Dr. Marius Barbeau, a distinguished Indian and Inuit anthropologist.

It was not until June 5, 1967, that Hattersley-Smith, together with a Royal Air Force party under Wing Commander D. le R. Bird, finally climbed to the highest point. On that day a group of nine climbed Barbeau Peak by three different routes: the north ridge, the west ridge and the south ridge. Hattersley-Smith left a note in a small cairn at the last rock, a few metres below the summit on the south ridge. Calculations, after correcting for temperature and air pressure, gave an elevation of 2600 m (8540 ft.) for Barbeau Peak, a little lower than previously thought, but without a doubt the highest peak in the Canadian Arctic.

Allan Errington led the next major expedition to the range in 1982. Errington's party landed on the ice cap near Mount Whisler, then worked its way southwest, climbing and naming every mountain in the ridge. But on a map published in the *American Alpine Journal*, Errington placed Barbeau Peak at a different location than had G. Hattersley-Smith. The peak Hattersley-Smith identified as Barbeau, Errington had named "Victory." This article and map caused considerable confusion regarding the proper location and identity of Barbeau Peak.

The most difficult part of an ascent of Barbeau Peak is the approach. Barbeau Peak is about 65 km (40.5 mi.) from Lake Hazen camp and about 90 km (56 mi.) from Tanquary Fiord. These are the only two established airstrips nearby. Also, Lake Hazen camp may not be suitable for departure, as its short runway limits payload for takeoff. It may be possible to land at Lake Hazen, climb to the peak, then descend to Tanquary Fiord for the return flight, but this would be a long and arduous journey. Another, and much more practical approach, is to land on the ice cap using aircraft equipped for ski landing, climb Barbeau Peak, then fly back. The climb could be done in this way in only two or three days. But anyone using this approach would miss a rare opportunity to experience a remarkable and inspiring landscape. Perhaps the best compromise is to land on the ice cap, climb Barbeau Peak, then hike out to Tanquary Fiord. A few parties have done this, and this is the route described below.

First, book a commercial flight to Resolute. This requires some planning as the options are limited. Canadian North flies to Resolute from Edmonton on Tuesdays and Saturdays, while First Air flies to Resolute from Ottawa on Wednesdays and Fridays. Reservations should be made early as the flights are commonly filled and low fares sell out quickly. Unfortunately, the need for early reservations conflicts with the need to ride-share the charter flight from Resolute to Ellesmere Island. The charter flight is expensive, about CAN $20,000 return. But this can be nearly cut in half by sharing the outbound flight with another party returning on the same day, and by sharing the return

Looking west across the ice cap from above Ekblaw Lake toward Barbeau Peak (indicated by the arrow). Photo Tony Daffern.

flight with another party coming in. This can generally be arranged through the charter flight service, but sometimes flexibility is needed in the schedule.

Resolute is no place to hang your hat for long. There is virtually no entertainment in the small village, and the land surrounding it is stark and barren. If time permits, a side trip can be arranged to Beechey Island, the wintering site of Sir John Franklin's ill-fated 1845 expedition, about 100 km (62.5 mi.) away. Archeological sites of Thule tent rings are located about 5 km (3 mi.) from the airstrip, and two rings have been reconstructed with rocks and whalebone to illustrate living conditions more than 500 years ago.

Everything in Resolute is very expensive. There are two places of lodging: the Qausuittuq Inn (formerly known as the High Arctic) that charges $185 per person per night, and the Narwhale Inn that charges $240 per person per night. In both cases this price includes transportation to and from the airport plus meals. Even at this price, accommodation is very basic with small rooms and shared bathrooms. The Qausuittuq Inn is the more nostalgic of the two, and has an interesting library complete with accounts of historic expeditions. At these rates, the lodging looks like a much better deal after the expedition rather than before it. There are no campgrounds in Resolute, but one can set up a tent almost anywhere outside the airport grounds.

There is a Tudjaat Co-op store in Resolute where groceries and basic items can be purchased, but here again prices are high. Visitors should have an ample supply of cash, as credit cards are not widely accepted.

Both First Air and Ken Borek Air provide charter flights from Resolute to Ellesmere Island using twin engine Otters. Maximum payload for this aircraft is about 1090 kg (2400 lbs.). This will generally accommodate up to 10 climbers together with gear and supplies. If the party is small, it may be possible to link up with another small party to make a full load. Most of the passengers to Ellesmere Island hike the Muskox Passage from Lake Hazen to Tanquary Fiord in about 10 days. Again, the charter service can be helpful in making contacts to facilitate ride-shares.

If it is necessary to land on the ice cap (and this is recommended for a climb of Barbeau Peak), the landing must be done early in the summer before the snow becomes soft and sticky. June 15 is usually the latest date that a charter service will guarantee a landing on the ice cap, although it has been done as late as June 30. Unfortunately, June is early for most of the visitors to Ellesmere Island, which makes arranging a ride-share all the more difficult.

Aircraft equipped for a ski landing can land either south or north of Barbeau Peak. Barbeau, together with the surrounding mountains are less steep on the north, and this is the recommended approach. Usually a landing on the north side can be made close enough so that the landing site can also serve as a summit camp from which the peak can be climbed in a single day.

The highest summit is the one immediately above the words "Barbeau Peak" on the 1:250,000 scale map Tanquary Fiord. Approach the peak up the valley immediately north-northwest of the peak. The approach is not difficult, consisting of a series of gradually ascending snow slopes leading to the foot of the peak. The last 300-400 m (1000-1300 ft.) of the approach are steeper, but not technically difficult. Crampons are needed for the final 50 m (160 ft.) up a moderate ice slope and finally along a sharp snow ridge to the top. Once on the summit, a small cairn and register can be found a few metres down at the highest rocks on the south ridge.

Return to camp by the same route in reverse.

After climbing the highpoint, there are several possible routes for descent from the ice cap. The route most often used is to head west for about 15 km (9 mi.), then gradually tend south, heading for the Air Force Glacier. Head down the Air Force Glacier for about 35 km (22 mi.), keeping near the left side of the glacier near the bottom. The Air Force Glacier is not steep, and crevasses are few and far between. A few side peaks along the way offer tempting opportunities for additional ascents.

As the toe of the glacier is approached, a rocky mountain on the left stands as a nunatak, separating the glaciers that flow around it from left and right. Where the two glaciers meet, glacier runoff collects in a rushing current that heads down to the Air Force River. Stay 100-200 m (330-650 ft.) away from the mountain and contour left toward the runoff channel. Here meltwater channels will be encountered. These channels range from tiny rivulets to rushing streams 1-3 m (3-10 ft.) across. The meltwater channels, which increase in size and strength as the summer progresses, can be difficult to cross. Once across the meltwater channels, exit from the glacier is easy, staying relatively close to the main current that empties into the river. It is not recommended to follow the glacier farther southwest toward the toe, as high ice cliffs and meltwater channels will complicate an exit from the glacier.

A variation of this descent route can be taken by heading directly southwest from the summit camp, passing between the mountains identified as "Intrepid" and "Blossom" on Allan Errington's map. This route is slightly shorter and steeper than the route previously described. In this case, the exit from the glacier will be down the east side of the nunatak and across on the other side of the main runoff channel described above.

The final barrier to the land is the Air Force River itself. The size and power of the river will vary depending on the season, but can generally be crossed without difficulty. The river here has the unusual feature of having a riverbed of smooth, slippery ice. It is therefore highly recommended to wear crampons for this crossing. If the river is swift, it may also be useful to cross in tandem or use a rope for safety.

Once across the Air Force River, head downstream toward Tanquary Fiord, staying on the left bank. Travel down the Air Force River valley is relatively easy, and sighting of muskox is not uncommon. Two more rivers, the Rollrock River and the Macdonald River, must be crossed before reaching Tanquary Fiord, but these present no greater difficulty than the previous crossing. This route is about 75 km (47 mi.) from peak to fiord. Parks headquarters are at GR 686386 (south of the "abandoned" camp).

In Tanquary Fiord, a bunkhouse, a cookhouse and a small visitor centre are at the disposal of guests, making waiting for the return flight pleasant indeed.

It is also possible to descend the ice cap south from Barbeau Peak. A group led by Les and Bev Wilson in 1996 traversed over the saddle immediately southwest of Barbeau Peak to reach the southern slopes. They described a difficult descent on the far side of the saddle down steep, icy slopes in high wind. The party then continued south down the ice cap to an exit on the Adams Glacier, where they encountered challenging meltwater channels. Once off the ice, they followed a route along Atka Lake down the Lewis River valley, and finally through the Macdonald River drainage to Tanquary Fiord. It is also possible, as a variation of this route, to descend and exit the Charybdis Glacier east of Ekblaw Lake. But in this event, it is still necessary to turn southeast and descend to the Macdonald River valley, as the Rollrock River valley is not a suitable route. The Macdonald River valley is part of the Lake Hazen-Tanquary Fiord corridor, known as the Muskox Passage. This corridor was used for centuries by the native Inuit in their migrations to and from Greenland, and was later used by Robert E. Peary in his quest for the North Pole. Both of these routes south to the Macdonald River have the disadvantage of being longer, about 100 km (62.5 mi.) from peak to fiord.

There is little reason for concern about the return flight to Resolute. It is highly unlikely that a flight to or from Ellesmere Island would be delayed owing to bad weather. Weather conditions are usually good, except for occasional high wind. Ellesmere Island is, in fact, a polar desert, one of the driest areas in the northern hemisphere, with an annual precipitation of only 6 cm (2.5 in.) per year. In such a place, it is important to make as little impact on the land as possible. Avoid disturbing vegetation, and respect wildlife from a distance. Careless travel in this sensitive place can leave scars that will last for centuries. This area of Ellesmere Island became Quttinirtaaq National Park in July 1999 and you should contact park personnel prior to the trip for the latest requlations. Hopefully, Ellesmere Island will remain a world apart for generations to come.

Contacts

Nunavut Tourism
P.O. Box 1450, Iqaluit, NWT XOA OHO
Phone: 867-979-6551 or 1-800-491-7910

Quttinirtaaq National Park
P.O. Box 353, Pangnirtung, NWT XOA ORO
Phone: 867-473-8828

First Air
P.O. Box 150, Resolute Bay, NWT XOA OVO
Phone: 867-252-3981

Ken Borek Air, Ltd.
290 McTavish Road N.E., Hanger #4, Calgary, AB T2E 7G5
Phone: 403-291-3300 or 867-252-3849

Qausuittuq Inns North
P.O. Box 270, Resolute Bay, NWT XOA OVO
Phone: 867-252-3900

Additional Reading

"British Empire Range, Ellesmere Island," Allan Errington, *American Alpine Journal*, 1983, p. 175-178. (Editor's note: The map contained in this article is not accurate and shows Barbeau Peak in the wrong position. Also note that the names given to peaks by the Errington party are not official.)

Geographical Names of the Ellesmere Island National Park Reserve and Vicinity, Geoffrey Hattersley-Smith, The Arctic Institute of North America.

The 1998 Nunavut Handbook, Nortext Multimedia Inc., Iqaluit, 1997.

Mont d'Iberville & Mount Caubvick

Québec & Newfoundland

Mont d'Iberville (Québec)
1652 m (5420 ft.)
Mount Caubvick (Newfoundland)
1653 m (5423 ft.)
Lat/long N58° 53' 17" W63° 42' 45"
UTM 458850m.E. 6527500m.N. (NAD 27)
Topo maps 14 L/13 Cirque Mountain
and 14 M/4 Nachvak Fiord

The rugged Torngat Mountains straddle the Newfoundland/Québec border on a narrow peninsula between the Atlantic Ocean on the east and Ungava Bay on the west. Within the Torngats, the Selamuit Range contains the highest peaks in eastern Canada south of Baffin Island. These mountains were a place of mystery and magic to the early Inuit. "Torngat" means "place of the devil" in Inuktitut. "Selamuit" literally means "sky-dwellers," but is used by the Inuit to refer to the northern lights, which they believe to be the dancing spirits of the dead. The mountains here are barren, being far north of the boreal forest of the east, but have a stark, desolate beauty that is usually accentuated by unsettled weather. Access to these remote peaks is difficult, and the climbing season is short.

These ancient mountains began forming 400 million years ago when North America was still connected to Europe. In fact, Labrador was joined to Scotland, which accounts for the similar topography, complete with rugged, barren mountains and deep fiords. When continental drift separated Europe from America, the Torngat Mountains were left standing at the northern end of the Appalachian mountain chain.

Prior to 1971 it was assumed that the highest peak east of the Rockies and south of Baffin Island was Cirque Mountain, a large mountain east of the Selamuit Range. Cirque Mountain was assigned an altitude of 1676 m (5500 ft.), a reading obtained with a pocket altimeter by A. P. Coleman when he made the first ascent in 1916. But in 1971 government cartographers working from aerial photographs demoted Cirque Mountain to 1568 m (5144 ft.), while at the same time contouring two other unnamed peaks greater than 1585 m (5200 ft.). One of these peaks, which overlooked the Tallek Arm of Nachvak Fiord, was given a reading of 1595 m (5232 ft.) on the 1:50,000 map Cirque Mountain. The other, a few kilometres inland on the Québec-Labrador border, was not further defined, but subsequent *Canada Yearbooks* assigned it an altitude of 1588 m (5210 ft.).

In August of 1971 the boundary peak was christened "Mont d'Iberville" by the Commission de Toponymie du Québec in honour of Pierre Le Moyne d'Iberville. This angered residents of Newfoundland as Moyne d'Iberville had led many ruthless expeditions against the English, including a particularly destructive rampage in St. John's and on the Avalon Peninsula of Newfoundland in 1696-7. But so long as the higher peak was assumed to be the unnamed mountain overlooking Nachvak Fiord safely within Newfoundland territory, the name did not seem of great importance.

"Mont d'Iberville" was first climbed in 1973 by Christopher Goetze and Michael Adler, two tough Americans who had kayaked north from Nain to Saglek Fiord, packing overland to the mountain. Then in 1975 Adler and four others sailed into Nachvak Fiord and climbed the unnamed 1595 m-high (5232 ft.) peak from Tallek Arm. Ray Chipeniuk and Ron Wilson, who named the peak "Torngarsoak Mountain," after the chief of the Torngait, or gods of the north Labrador Inuit, made the first Canadian ascent of this peak in 1977. Chipeniuk and Wilson believed that they had climbed the highest peak of the Torngats.

After returning to Ottawa, one of these climbers chanced upon an old map that showed Mont d'Iberville to have an elevation of 1622 m (5320 ft.). Surprised and disturbed, he contacted the Surveys and Mapping Branch of the Ministry of Energy, Mines and Resources. After setting up their photogrammetry equipment to have another look, the mapmakers were surprised to find elevation readings on Mont d'Iberville all the way up to 1665 m (5464 ft.). The last 150 m (500 ft.) of the sharp spire were nearly straight up on all four sides, and well above the challenge of Torngarsoak Mountain. Eastern Canada therefore had a higher and more spectacular peak than anyone had imagined. Furthermore, this peak had been climbed only once, by Americans.

These revelations led to a Canadian expedition organized for August of 1978, with its primary objective an ascent of Mont d'Iberville. The expedition landed at the mouth of the McCornik River in Nachvak Fiord, and after making its way south, succeeded in making several first ascents in the Selamuit Range. Finally, Mont d'Iberville was climbed via the Minaret Spur and Minaret Ridge by Ray Chipeniuk, Ron Parker and Erik Sheer on August 14, 1978. After climbing to the top amid windblown frost feathers, the three climbers noticed something surprising. The so-called "Mont d'Iberville" was in fact an intersection of three sharp ridges. Along two of these ridges, the Minaret and the Korok, ran the Québec-Newfoundland border. About 10 m (30 ft.) north on the third ridge, and well inside Newfoundland territory, was the true summit of the mountain. This point was a little more than a metre above anything in Québec.

The climbers reported their findings to the Newfoundland Department of Tourism, and in 1981 the Newfoundland Geographical Names Board decided that the mountain should have an English name more suitable to the region's history. The board therefore gave it the name of Mount Caubvick in honour of one of the five Inuit who accompanied George Cartwright, a trader on the Labrador coast, to England in 1772. And so it is that the highest peak in eastern Canada south of Baffin Island has two very different names and two slightly different elevations, even though it is, in fact, the same mountain.

By 1982, Mont d'Iberville/Mount Caubvick had been climbed six times by the Minaret Ridge, but the north ridge and the long Koroc Ridge had not yet been climbed. In July of that year Timothy Keliher and Hazen Russel made the first ascent of the steep north ridge, unofficially called the Newfoundland Ridge as it lies entirely within the province of Newfoundland.

(Much of the above historical account is taken from a report, "1978 Torngat Mountain Expedition," written for the Newfoundland Department of Tourism.)

Koroc Ridge

The long Koroc Ridge is the most prominent feature on the mountain. This ridge runs south, at first along the Québec-Newfoundland border, then farther south toward the Koroc River. The Koroc Ridge is seldom climbed, as the usual approach to the mountain is from Nachvak Fiord and the McCornik River.

The Koroc Ridge may be approached from either the Tallek Arm of Nachvak Fiord or from the Koroc River. From Tallek Arm, the Palmer River may be followed south about 5 km (3 mi.) to a small creek that leads east toward Mont d'Iberville. The upper portion of the Koroc Ridge may be reached by ascending to the headwaters of this small creek. This has apparently been done, but is not reported in the climbing literature. The Koroc Ridge may also be approached from a landing site along the Koroc River at N58° 46' 30" W63° 35' 30" at an elevation of about 260 m (850 ft.). This site is a natural gravel bar used by Air Inuit, which flies twin engine DeHaviland Otters equipped with tundra tires. The gravel bar is only 15 km (9 mi.) southeast of the summit of Mont d'Iberville. Air Inuit flies out of Kuujjuaq, Québec, which is in turn serviced by scheduled commercial flights from Montréal. It should also

The summit ridge. Photo Tony Daffern.

be possible to fly from Kuujjuaq and land by floatplane on Tallek Arm, but charter services in Kuujjuaq are reluctant to do this, especially in August when hunting and fishing charters are at their peak. The approach from the gravel bar along the Koroc River is the one described below.

The landing site is about 200 m (650 ft.) south of the Koroc River. The river is shallow near the landing site, and may be crossed easily by wading between sandbars. Continue downriver to a point about 1 km (0.6 mi.) downstream from where the stream draining the south side of Mont d'Iberville joins the Koroc River. From here ascend the gently sloping valley northwest to a small lake at the foot of the Koroc Ridge. The lake is about 10 km (6 mi.) and 300 m (1000 ft.) higher than the river. The lake, at N58° 51' 00" W63° 43' 20" and at an elevation of about 560 m (1850 ft.), makes a good campsite for an attempt on the summit.

Climb the small snow couloir north of the lake to the prominent shoulder that overlooks the valley. Now bear northeast to attain the ridgecrest. From here the final sharp summit of Mont d'Iberville finally comes into view. Follow the ridgecrest to the intersection of another ridge from the west. This is the watershed divide that separates Québec from Newfoundland. Continue toward the summit along this ridge, which becomes narrower as the peak is approached. Two cairns are built at a prominent knob in the ridge. The ridge north of this knob is separated from the main peak by a deep notch, formed where a conspicuous dike cuts through the ridgeline. Beyond the knob the ridge becomes airy and exposed, and is crowned with several pinnacles. Most of these pinnacles can be passed without difficulty, but the final one, leading down to the dike notch, is much more difficult. Rappel down the face of this pinnacle to the notch. Most experienced climbers will not regard the rest of the ascent as difficult, so the rappel rope may be left in place to be used as a top belay during the return.

Unlike the rocks of the ridge, which are hard granite and gneiss, the rocks in the dike notch are softer red and brown volcanic intrusion. Foot and handholds in the notch are often loose and unstable, so caution is well advised. The first orange-brown pinnacle in the notch can be passed on the right.

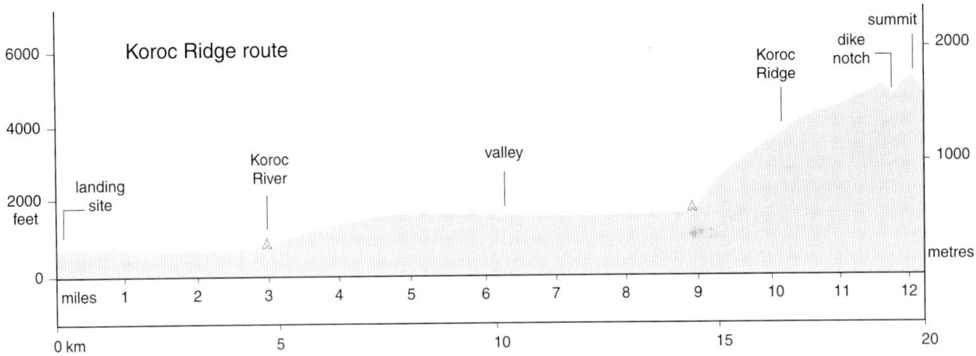

Mont d'Iberville/Mount Caubvick from the curving Koroc Ridge. Photo Tony Daffern.

The second orange pinnacle may be climbed by slipping down through a narrow "fat-man's misery" crack on the left. Once beyond the dike notch, the ridge above may be climbed with caution to the summit of Mont d'Iberville.

The "summit" of Mount Caubvick is 10 m (30 ft.) north along the summit ridge and is about 1 m (3 ft.) higher than that of d'Iberville.

From the summit of d'Iberville, retrace the ascent route in reverse to return to the summit camp by the lake. The rappel rope left at the dike pinnacle, which is the crux of the route, may be conveniently used as a top belay for the return.

Minaret Ridge

The Minaret Ridge was the first ascent route on the mountain, and is still the most commonly used path to the summit. The approach begins in the little fishing village of Nain on the Labrador coast. Nain can be reached by scheduled commercial flights that operate daily from Goose Bay. Tom Goodwin runs high-speed boats up the Labrador coast from Atsinik Lodge to Nachvak Fiord. The boats carry up to eight passengers and fill up quickly, so early reservations are recommended. The trip to Nachvak is nearly 400 km (240 mi.), and takes the better part of two days. The scenery and wildlife up the Labrador coast are probably worth the trip alone. Nachvak Fiord itself may be cluttered with icebergs, depending on the season and the year.

Once in Nachvak Fiord, put ashore on the east side of the broad river delta created by the McCornik River. From this point it is 9 km (6 mi.) to the first feasible base camp for a summit attempt. Caribou trails are plentiful and the hiking is easy. The only serious problem is crossing the

McCornik River, together with the various glacier brooks that charge down from the surrounding heights. These torrents can be intimidating, but are less difficult in the mornings when less meltwater is present. The brooks along the east side of the McCornik River are smaller, at least up to Cirque Brook. Ford the McCornik River somewhere below Cirque Brook. The second ascent party in 1978 made their base camp on a broad step in the tundra along the McCornik River just across from Cirque Brook. The summit of Mont d'Iberville is still about 8 km (5 mi.) from here, however, and a higher camp may be sensible. From this point, the climb to the summit and return took the 1978 party 15 hours.

The next stream that enters the McCornik River is d'Iberville Brook. Follow d'Iberville Brook through gentle caribou pastures, then up steeper and rockier ground above 460 m (1500 ft.). Pass Stone Ring Falls, a phenomenal torrent with two concentric rings of rubble and a deep sparkling moat between them. It is also possible to site a summit camp above Stone Ring Falls at an elevation of about 700 m (2300 ft.). From here the summit is only about 4 km (2.5 mi.) distant.

Continue up d'Iberville Brook to attain the Minaret Glacier. From the glacier, climb onto the Minaret Spur via the lateral moraine that flanks the glacier on the west. Continue up the Minaret Spur to its intersection with the Minaret Ridge, the main ridge leading southeast from the peak. There are one or two steep steps on the Minaret Spur, but these can be climbed without difficulty. At this intersection is a cairn, presumably erected by the first ascent party.

The Minaret Ridge is very exposed, and crowned with many pinnacles and gendarmes. The ridge is especially steep on the north end where it drops sharply to Ice-Blue Tarn, but is gentler on the south side where it gives way to a system of ledges and broken blocks of rock. Confident rock climbers used to exposure may choose to do this section unroped, but an occasional belay for safety will be needed for others. The hardest climbing on the ridge has been rated at 5.2 by the 1978 expedition. Continue along the Minaret Ridge to the summit of Mont d'Iberville. From here, the "summit" of Mount Caubvick is reached by walking about 10 m (30 ft.) north along the north ridge into Newfoundland territory.

Return to summit camp by climbing down the Minaret Ridge, Minaret Spur and d'Iberville Brook, retracing the ascent route in reverse.

Another possible route

From the summit of Mont d'Iberville it appears that an easier route might exist from the south. A small unnamed lake lies south-southeast just below the d'Iberville summit. The unclimbed ridge to the east of this lake looks as if it could be climbed without difficulty to the point where it intersects with the Minaret Ridge. From this intersection, the upper portion of the Minaret Ridge can be taken to the top.

To return to civilization, one can either arrange a flight back to Kuujjuaq from the same landing site used for the approach, or float down the Koroc River to a point where the return flight is shorter and less expensive. The latter option adds variety to the trip and is definitely more interesting. But to attempt the Koroc, climbers must also be competent white-water boaters. The Koroc River descends steeply to the sea, and includes several rapids up to Class V in difficulty, as well as one large waterfall. The river may be boated with either inflatable craft or canoe, but considerable skill is needed to navigate the Koroc by canoe. A detailed description of the river and its hazards is given in the narrative section of this book.

Contacts

Tourisme Québec
Case postale 20 000, Québec City, PQ G1K 7X2
Phone: 1-800-363-7777

Johnny May's Air Charter
Phone: Kuujjuaq 819-964-2662, Stewart Lake 819-964-2321

Air Inuit
1985 – 55th Avenue, Dorval, PQ H6P 1G9
Phone: 514-636-9445, fax: 514-636-4513

Co-op Hotel, Kuujjuaq. Phone: 819-964-2272

Newfoundland Deptartment of Tourism and Culture
P.O. Box 8730, St. John's, NFLD A1B 4K2
Phone: 1-800-563-6353

Atsanik Lodge
P.O. Box 10, Nain, LB AOP 1LO
Phone: 709-922-2910, fax: 709-922-2815

Tom Goodwin Holdings
Nain, LB AOP 1LO.
Phone: 709-922-2812

Additional Reading

"1978 Torngat Mountain Expedition," report to the Newfoundland Department of Tourism, 1978.
"The 1980 Torngat Expedition: By Kayak Along the Labrador Coast," Eric Radak, *Appalachia Journal*, 1981, p. 9-27.
"First Newfoundland Ascent of Caubvick," R. J. Rogerson, *Canadian Alpine Journal,* 1983.

White Hill

Nova Scotia

532 m (1747 ft.)
Lat/long N46° 42' 08" W60° 35' 55"
UTM 683500m.E. 5174750m.N. (NAD 27)
Topo maps 11 K/9 Ingonish
and 11 K/10 Chéticamp River

At the northeast tip of Nova Scotia is a land of rugged ocean coastline, waterfalls, sandy beaches and pristine mountain highlands. Whales play in the waters offshore and bald eagles soar in the coastal breezes. It is also a place of rich cultural history; inhabited by Scottish, Irish, Acadian and Mi'kmaq peoples. You may hear conversations in English, French or even Gaelic. This is Cape Breton Island, and Cape Breton Highlands National Park.

Cape Breton Highlands National Park protects 950 sq. km (594 sq. mi.) of magnificent coastline and mountain wilderness. The inhabitants of Cape Breton Island have settled near the sea, and left the mountain highlands virtually untouched. As the traveller climbs from the coastline high into the hills, majestic forest gives way to stunted spruce, alders and open bogs. The brush is dense; and at times seems almost impenetrable. This is no place to bushwhack cross-country. If the unwary traveller loses the trail and becomes disoriented, recovery will be no easy matter.

White Hill is deep in the Cape Breton Highlands, and no maintained trail leads to it. The trails shown on the topographic maps of the region are in reality old fire roads that have not been maintained since the advent of aircraft for fire monitoring and control. Some of these old fire roads are practically impossible to follow.

There are two possible approaches to White Hill; the Franey Mountain trail, and Lake of Islands trail. Both options are very long one-day hikes, and are probably better attempted in two days with an overnight camp. In either case, the hiker must be continually aware of his location, and be skilled in compass and cross-country travel.

Franey Mountain Trail

The Franey Mountain trail to White Hill is a rugged, unmaintained fire road. It is badly overgrown with spruce and alder and is at times difficult to follow. The old road has all but disappeared where it crosses open bogs and meadows. Extreme caution is needed to stay on the trail and avoid getting lost in the bush.

Turn left on the road to the Franey Mountain fire lookout about 3 km (2 mi.) north of Ingonish Beach on the Cabot Trail Highway. This dirt road leads steeply uphill for 2 km (1.25 mi.) to a parking area at the Cape Breton Highlands National Park boundary at an elevation of about 170 m (560 ft.). From this trailhead, a well-maintained trail leads 4 km (2.5 mi.) to a fire lookout. About 2.5 km (1.5 mi.) up this trail, at an elevation of about 370 m (1210 ft.), a faint fire road branches off to the right. Follow this trail west through dense spruce and alder bush.

About 9 km (5.5 mi.) from the trailhead, the old road enters open boggy meadows. Here the road all but disappears and caution should be used to memorize or mark the trail for the return trip. After the meadows the canopy opens up and the old road becomes easier to follow.

A major junction of fire roads is reached about 13 km (8 mi.) from the trailhead. The fire road leading northeast from this junction leads to the Lake of Islands trail and campground. This junction is at an elevation of about 470 m (1550 ft.). Continue west-northwest through the junction another 3 km. White Hill will be visible to the left beyond White Hill Lake.

At the highest point on the fire road, and due north of White Hill, leave the road and bushwhack directly for the summit about 0.75 km (.5 mi.) away. This bushwhack through dense low growth is very strenuous, especially near the fire road, but opens up as elevation is gained. A square concrete block and survey marker mark the rounded summit, and a fallen red-and-white radio tower lies victim to the elements. The views across the highlands are outstanding from the summit.

Follow the same route in reverse to return to the Franey Mountain trailhead, being careful to stay on the trail. The entire trip makes a long day, covering about 33 km (20 mi.) with an elevation gain of about 360 m (1180 ft.).

Lake of Islands Trail

The Lake of Islands trail is probably the best approach to White Hill, despite being the longer route. The total round-trip distance is 43.5 km (27 mi.), but 25.8 km (16 mi.) are on a well-maintained trail, leaving only 17.7 km (11 mi.) of unmaintained fire road and bushwhacking to negotiate. Also, the fire road from Lake of Islands is easier to stay on than the fire road past Franey Mountain. Furthermore, there is a designated wilderness campsite at Lake of Islands, which serves as a convenient overnight stopover.

To get to the Lake of Islands trail, follow the Cabot Trail Highway to the Broad Cove area, about 3 km (2 mi.) north of Ingonish. From there, turn onto the dusty, gravel Mary Ann Falls road and follow it north through forest for about 4.5 km (2.8 mi.). Then turn left on a steep and rutted spur road that leads to a small parking area at the Lake of Islands trailhead, at an elevation of about 110 m (360 ft.). This road is well signed and should not pose a problem for passenger vehicles.

The Lake of Islands trail is a regularly maintained path that leads to its namesake 12.9 km (8 mi.) from the trailhead. The first few kilometres are steady uphill, but not steep, and views of the ocean behind are spectacular. A small spur path leads to Branch Pond about 6.5 km (4 mi.) from the trailhead. Finally, only about 0.5 km (0.3 mi.) before reaching Lake of Islands, there is an unsigned junction with an old fire road leading left. Turn southwest on this road.

From the Lake of Islands trail junction, the old road is often overgrown and boggy, but still provides relatively easy going. There is a warden cabin on the left, overlooking swampy Tipover Lake about 2.8 km (1.75 mi.) after leaving the Lake of Islands trail. The road gets progressively muddy and overgrown as it continues southwest, and two brook crossings are thick with vegetation and difficult to plow through.

A four-way junction of fire roads is reached about 6.3 km (4 mi.) from Lake of Islands trail, and about 18.3 km (11.5 mi.) from the trailhead, at an elevation of about 470 m (1550 ft.). This is the same major junction described in the above section. Turn right at this junction, heading west-northwest, and follow the description under Franey Mountain trail for the rest of the way to White Hill summit.

Follow the same route in reverse to return to Lake of Islands and Lake of Islands trailhead. It is probably not a good idea to return by the Franey Mountain trail, which would be unfamiliar and difficult to follow.

The Lake of Islands trail is a designated bike path, which presents another prospect for a one-day trip. It should be possibile to rent a mountain bike from one of the local cycle shops and ride the bike to Lake of Islands. This leaves only about 17.7 km (11 mi.) round-trip for the hike to White Hill. Of course, cycling to a highpoint may offend the sensibility of some, but this is a difficult trek and a not a bad place for bending the rules.

Contacts

Department of Tourism and Culture
P.O. Box 130, Halifax, NS B3J 2M7
Phone: 1-800-341-6096

Cape Breton Highlands National Park
Ingonish Beach, NS B0C 1L0
Phone: 902-285-2691 or 902-224-3403
Fax: 902-285-2866

Mount Carleton

New Brunswick

820 m (2690 ft.)
Lat/long N47° 22' 39" W66° 52' 35"
UTM 660200m.E. 5249150m.N. (NAD 27)
Topo map 21 O/7 Nepisiguit Lakes

The highpoint of New Brunswick is Mount Carleton, a treeless rocky summit rising well above the neighbouring hills. The wind on the peak may be chilling, but the view is worthwhile. Mount Carleton, sitting astride the Saint John/Nepisiguit watershed divide, is the highest peak in the Maritime provinces. The lonely tower perched on top was home to men who operated the Mount Carleton fire tower from 1923 until 1968.

The rocks of Mount Carleton were formed during the early Devonian period, about 400 million years ago. During that time, the area that was to become Mount Carleton Provincial Park was a marine basin. This marine basin was uplifted as the continental landmass from the east collided with the Canadian Shield, producing the Appalachian mountain chain. These mountains originally rivalled the Himalayas in height. But for most of the last 400 million years Mount Carleton has undergone weathering and erosion, reducing the initially lofty peaks to their present height. Occasional periods of volcanic activity deposited the volcanic rocks within the park today. The volcanic rocks of Mount Carleton are a hard, resistant type of rhyolite, containing crystals of pink feldspar.

W. F. Ganong determined New Brunswick's highest elevation in 1899 and named it Mount Carleton in honour of Thomas Carleton, the first lieutenant governor of New Brunswick. Beginning in 1923, Mount Carleton was the summer home of the towermen, who scanned the forest for smoke from the glassed-in top of the tower. If they spotted smoke, they would use a crank telephone to call headquarters with a bearing and estimated distance. The towermen lived in a small cabin in the woods a few hundred metres down the trail. The tower and cabin were no longer manned after 1968, when airplanes began to be used for patrolling.

To approach Mount Carleton, first drive north on Highway 385, east of Grand Falls, New Brunswick. Continue north on Highway 385 for 28 km (17.5 mi.) past Nictau to Nictau Lake in Mount Carleton Provincial Park. Turn east along the shore of Nictau Lake. After about 3 km (2 mi.), turn south on a dirt road that leads up Bald Mountain Brook. Continue on this road about 8 km (5 mi.) to the parking lot at the Mount Carleton trailhead.

Two trails lead from the trailhead to the summit of Mount Carleton. The east trail, 4.4 km long (2.75 mi.), is the standard approach and is the trail most used. The west trail, 5.2 km (3.25 mi.) to the summit, leads past the "headwaters" backcountry campground, then on to the peak. These two trails make a nice circle route if you ascend the east trail, then return via the west trail.

The east trail follows an old road as it climbs gently through mature spruce and fir mixed with yellow birch. The trail turns sharply left at 2.8 km (1.75 mi.) at the Big Brook trail junction, and becomes steeper and rockier. The towermen's cabin is just beyond this turn. Supplies were brought up this road to the cabin where the fire towermen sheltered during storms or when off duty. Just beyond the cabin the peak of Mount Carleton finally comes into view. The final few hundred metres to the summit are steep and rocky, but not difficult. The total elevation gain from the trailhead is 400 m (1300 ft.).

The view from the summit is enjoyable in good weather. Mount Sagamook and Mount Head are north, Nepisiguit Lakes east, Mount Bailey northwest, and the Serpentine Mountains to the southwest. Mountain cranberries and blueberries are plentiful on the peak in September.

To complete the circle route back to the trailhead, continue past the fire tower on the west trail. In bad weather, an alternative side path beyond the fire tower allows a quick exit from the exposed ridgecrest. After about 1.5 km (.9 mi.), nestled beside three beaver ponds, is the "headwaters" backcountry campground. From the campground there is an excellent view of Mount Carleton. An optional and rugged 2 km-long (1.25 mi.) loop side trail leads over Mount Carleton's twin peak. The main trail descends along a brook, then swings south across the hillside to the parking lot. Hiking time for the entire loop is an easy three hours.

Contacts

Tourism New Brunswick, Dept. 339
P.O. Box 12345, Fredericton, NB E3B 5C3
Phone: 1-800-561-0123

Mount Carleton Provincial Park
P.O. Box 1567, 35 Principal Street, Saint Jacques, NB E7B 1A3
Phone: 506-235-2025 or 1-800-561-0123

Ishpatina Ridge
Ontario

693 m (2275 ft.)
Lat/long N47° 19' 00" W80° 45' 05"
UTM 518800m.E. 5240450m.N. (NAD 83)
Topo map 41 P/7 Smoothwater Lake

The core of ancient rock beneath each continental plate is called a "shield." In North America, this rock is called the "Canadian Shield" as a vast expanse of it lies exposed in central and northern Canada. The Canadian Shield contains the oldest rock in Canada, dating back 4,000 million years. The shield erodes so slowly that it has changed little in the past 500 million years. The landscape is dotted with crystalline lakes that seem to drain with no logical pattern. Forests of spruce, birch, maple and oak cling to the thin soil where it has collected between ridges of exposed granite. While other regions have undergone mountain building and wearing away, sometimes several times, this ancient and beautiful landscape has remained changeless for untold ages.

In the early 1960s, Tip Top Mountain near Lake Superior was considered the highest point in Ontario. In 1966, the distinction passed to Ogidaki Mountain near Sault St. Marie. Only in 1972 was it determined that a granite ridge 95 km (60 mi.) south of Sudbury was 28 m (92 ft.) higher. This is Ishpatina Ridge, a word that means "high hill" in the Ojibwa native language. Ishpatina Ridge, which runs for 12 km (7.5 mi.) from northeast to southwest, has several high humps that rise above the surrounding forest. Two of these humps, about 2 km (1.25 mi.) apart, lie above the 2250 foot contour line. The summit to the southwest is largely barren, and has an old fire tower on top. It has been reported that this is the higher of the two summits, but at the time of writing this has not been confirmed with certainty.

Ishpatina Ridge may be approached from either the north or south, and both routes have been used. The northern route through Smoothwater Lake requires travelling 28 km (17.5 mi.) by canoe, including six well-maintained portages, followed by a hike up a 5 km-long (3 mi.) trail. The southern route requires travelling 75 km (47 mi.) over logging roads, followed by several kilometres of difficult bushwhacking. It may be possible to substitute this bushwhack by a canoe trek over shallow creeks and lakes. A four-wheel-drive vehicle is recommended for the southern approach. Of the two options, the northern approach is probably the better choice.

Smoothwater Lake (northern approach)

From Elk Lake, Ontario, travel about 25 km (15.5 mi.) east on Highway 560 to Beauty Lake Road. Turn left off the paved highway and continue about 12 km (7.5 mi.) on Beauty Lake Road to the Isabel Lake junction. Turn right at the junction and travel another 10 km (6 mi.) to the Montréal River bridge.

Launch a canoe at the boat landing south of the Montréal River bridge and travel upriver about 4 km (2.5 mi.) to Lady Dufferin Lake. The Montréal River is narrow here, but except for one swift chute, the current is generally slow and easily paddled. Continue southeast 3 km (2 mi.) through Lady Dufferin Lake. Re-enter the Montréal River and paddle another 4 km (2.5 mi.) upriver to Smoothwater Lake.

Smoothwater Lake is 6 km (3.75 mi.) long and, contrary to its name, can be very rough in high winds, particularly those from the south. When the lake is rough, it is wise to follow close to the shore. Travel 6 km (3.75 mi.) south across Smoothwater Lake to a portage located at the extreme southern tip of the lake. The portage begins at an old lumber camp dock and runs 770 m (2526 ft.) to Apex Lake. There is a good campsite at the beginning of this portage, as well as at the northern end of Smoothwater Lake, and another halfway down Smoothwater on the east shore near the outlet from Marina Lake.

Cross the portage to Apex Lake. Apex Lake marks the height of land where waters to the north and east follow the Montréal River drainage system, and waters to the south flow into the Sturgeon River drainage. Paddle 1 km (0.6 mi.) to a portage heading south from the southeastern end of the lake (do not take another portage heading east). This 1110 m (3642 ft.) portage travels over a height of land and drops slightly to a small unnamed lake.

Paddle 400 m (1312 ft.) across this small lake to find a short 60 m (197 ft.) portage to another small pond. There is a good campsite at this portage. Paddle 200 m (656 ft.) across this pond to find another short portage, about 30 m (98.4 ft.) long, which leads around some shallows to yet another small unnamed lake. Paddle 600 m (1968 ft.) to the southern end of this lake to find a 150 m (492 ft.) portage to McCulloch Lake.

Paddle 1.7 km (1 mi.) south-southeast down McCulloch Lake to a final 105 m (344 ft.) portage at its southern outlet. Travel over this last portage, then continue through a narrow lake and down tiny Scarecrow Creek into Mihell Lake. Paddle southwest about 1.5 km (1 mi.) down Mihell Lake to find the entrance to Scarecrow Creek on the right shore.

This portion of Scarecrow Creek is the most difficult part of the route. The creek is very small here and meanders constantly through marsh and low brush. At times it is necessary to lift or push the canoe over beaver dams, fallen logs or rocky shallows. The difficulty of Scarecrow Creek will vary with the season and water level. The distance from Mihell Lake to Scarecrow Lake is only about 3 km (2 mi.), but seems much longer owing to the meandering and difficulty of the creek.

Once on Scarecrow Lake, continue along the west bank of the lake about 200 m (656 ft.) to the site of an old dock and warden cabin. Just north of this site is the trail that leads 5 km (3 mi.) to the fire tower at the top of Ishpatina Ridge. The trail, which is a little overgrown but not difficult to follow, leads steadily up past three isolated lakes and finally onto the open summit. The summit is mostly granite, covered with blueberry and a few twisted scrub oaks. The view from the top is spectacular over the numerous lakes and rocky knobs of Lady Evelyn-Smoothwater Provincial Park. The old fire tower is marked with a sign that reads "DO NOT CLIMB," good advice considering the obvious disrepair of the antiquated tower. Two km (1.25 mi.) northeast is another rise of Ishpatina Ridge that looks about as high, but is covered in brush and oak. There is no trail to this knob, and reaching it would involve tedious bushwhacking.

Return to Scarecrow Lake, Smoothwater Lake and the Montréal River by the same route in reverse. Returning up Scarecrow Creek is especially difficult against the current.

The entire trip from the Montréal River bridge to Ishpatina Ridge and return requires at least one camp along the way. A camp at the small unnamed lake south of Apex Lake is a good choice. This allows most of the distance to be covered the first day, with a trip to the highpoint and return to be made on the second day and a return to the put-in on the third day. Although long, about 66 km (41 mi.) round-trip, this journey is very enjoyable and unique among highpoint trips. The rhythm of silently paddling through these beautiful pristine lakes of the Canadian Shield is an experience that will not soon be forgotten.

Sturgeon River

From Sudbury, Ontario, travel north through Garson to Capreol. From just north of Capreol, an 80 km-long (50 mi.) logging road heads north into the Canadian wilderness. Follow this dirt road north along the Wanapitei River. Turn right on a small dirt road about 51 km (32 mi.) north of Capreol just before a bridge that crosses the Wanapitei River. Follow this small road another 18 km (11 mi.) past Brennan Lake and Dave Lake. This road is seldom travelled, and parts of it are classified as a "vehicle track." It may be advisable to use a four-wheel-drive vehicle for this approach.

Finally, the Sturgeon River is reached at a washed-out bridge. It has been reported that the Sturgeon River can be crossed with a four-wheel-drive utility vehicle if the water level is very low. If so, one could then drive another 5 km (3 mi.) past an old sawmill and across a low bridge over Scarecrow Creek to Stull Lake. If it is possible to drive this far, a 6 km (3.75 mi.) bushwhack can be made to the Ishpatina Ridge trailhead on the west bank of Scarecrow Lake, described above. If it is not possible to drive across the Sturgeon River, cross the river on foot and hike the additional 5 km (3 mi.) to Stull Lake. Bushwhacking through this country is tough going, however, and the 6 km (3.75 mi.) bushwhack can be expected to take three hours each way. A hike from the Sturgeon River can be expected to take at least nine hours round-trip.

Alternatively, from the low bridge over Scarecrow Creek, take a canoe and paddle east through a small unnamed lake to the continuation of Scarecrow Creek. Follow Scarecrow Creek about 1 km (0.6 mi.) upstream over four sets of gravel rapids, then across a 130 m (426 ft.) portage to Woods Lake. Paddle north 2.5 km (1.5 mi.) through Woods Lake, then 2 km (1.25 mi.) north on Scarecrow Lake to the Ishpatina Ridge trailhead.

If it is possible to cross the Sturgeon River by vehicle and drive as far as Scarecrow Creek, then the approach by canoe will be easy, probably taking not more than six hours round trip. But if the Sturgeon River cannot be crossed, then it will not be convenient to use a canoe from the south and this approach will be very difficult. The uncertainties of the southern approach, together with the charm of the route from the north, make this southern option my second choice.

Contacts

Travel Ontario
Phone: 1-800-668-2746 or 705-564-6019

Lady Evelyn-Smoothwater Provincial Park
Suite 901, 199 Larch Street, Sudbury, ON P3E 5P9
Phone: 705-564-6019

Additional Reading

"Temagami Canoe Routes," Hap Wilson, Ontario Ministry of Natural Resources, 1979, Route #20, Smoothwater Lake–Sturgeon River Route, p. 116-120.

Baldy Mountain

Manitoba

832 m (2729 ft.)
Lat/long N51° 28' 10" W100° 43' 10"
UTM 380500m.E. 5703300m.N. (NAD 27)
Topo map 62 N/7 Baldy Mountain

Baldy Mountain is the highest point on a long series of highlands known as the Manitoba Escarpment. It stands in the southeast corner of Duck Mountain Provincial Park, a land of rolling terrain, dense woodland forest, wetlands and deep blue lakes. The park is home to a variety of wildlife including black bear, moose, white-tailed deer, elk, lynx, coyote and wolves. When entering Duck Mountain Park from the vast plains of Manitoba, the boreal and deciduous forest closes behind like a great green curtain.

More than 70 million years ago, Manitoba was covered by a warm, shallow sea. Clay and silt settled to the sea floor and were compressed into marine sedimentary rocks. About 15 million years later these rocks were uplifted and subjected to the erosion of rivers and streams. The final sculpting was completed by ice, which last retreated some 15,000 years ago, leaving countless depressions in the surface where great lumps of ice were left behind. When these lumps of ice melted, they left hollows called "kettles." The kettles are now filled with run-off water or springs, forming a myriad of small ponds glittering in the sunlight.

From Grandview, Manitoba, travel north on Highway 366 for 30 km (20 mi.) to Duck Mountain Provincial Park. Continue another 2.5 km (1.5 mi.) to a point where a small dirt road branches off to the left. Take this small road 2 km (1.25 mi.) to the summit of Baldy Mountain. From the parking lot at the end of the road, a trail leads about 100 m (328 ft.) to a wooden observation tower. The tower offers a beautiful view of the hills and forest of Duck Mountain Park, as well as the boundless plains of Manitoba to the south.

Contacts

Manitoba Natural Resources
P.O. Box 22, Saulteaux Crescent,
Winnipeg, MB R3J 3W3
Phone: 204-945-6784 or 1-800-214-6497
Web site: www.gov.mb.ca/natres

Travel Manitoba, Deptartment AD5, 7th Floor
155 Carlton Street, Winnipeg, MB R3C 3H8
Phone: 204-945-3777 or 1-800-665-0040

Unnamed Point in the Cypress Hills

Saskatchewan

1392 m (4567 ft.)
Lat/long N49° 33' 07" W109° 59' 11"
UTM 573300m.E. 5489050m.N. (NAD 27)
Topo map 72 F/12 Hungerford Lakes

The Cypress Hills, rising nearly 600 m (2000 ft.) above the surrounding prairie, are the highest elevation between the foothills of the Canadian Rockies and the Torngat Mountains of Labrador. It is believed that the Cypress Hills stood like a nunatak during the Pleistocene Ice Age, with the giant glaciers flowing around its flanks. Covering about 2500 sq. km (1000 sq. mi.), the hills are now in the shape of a long plateau on the border between Saskatchewan and Alberta. The sides of the hills have been eroded into valleys and low hills, and are covered with lodgepole pine, spruce and aspen.

About 6 km (3.75 mi.) east of the Saskatchewan highpoint, tucked into a valley alongside the meandering Battle Creek, is Fort Walsh National Historic Site. Two km (1.25 mi.) downstream from the fort is Farwell's Trading Post, the site of an event that changed the course of Canadian history. In the early 1870s, the Cypress Hills were a haven used by the Blackfoot, Assiniboine and Plains Cree Indians. It was a sorry time on the northwest plains. Smallpox had ravaged the Plains Indians, and whisky trading posts were set up to bring further misery to the once prosperous natives. Tension between Indians and whites was at an all-time high.

Early in the spring of 1873, a party of American wolf hunters, or "wolfers" had about 40 horses stolen by Cree Indian raiders, and tracked the thieves to the Cypress Hills. Meanwhile, Indians camped near Farwell's Post were angry at the way white traders treated them, and had made numerous threats. Farwell put up the wolfers for the night and cracked open the whisky. By morning, June 1, both whites and Indians were in a drunken stupor, and a band of warriors, stripped for war, taunted the whites and brandished their weapons. It is not known for sure who fired the first shot, but by the next morning somewhere between 30 and 50 Assiniboines (including some women and children) had been slaughtered. The news of the massacre fanned the flames of nationalism and anti-Americanism in eastern Canada, and caused the federal government to push ahead with the formation of the North West Mounted Police to keep peace on the frontier.

Today little is left to suggest the mayhem and murder of 1873. The green curves of the Cypress Hills are a peaceful retreat for hunters and backpackers, and the home of ranchers and many species of wildlife, including lynx, bobcat, coyotes, elk and bison.

The highpoint of Saskatchewan can be approached by road to within a few hundred metres, although the road is not maintained and may be in poor condition.

Turn southwest from Maple Creek, Saskatchewan, on Highway 271, a hard surface two-lane road. After 44 km (27.5 mi.), where Highway 271 turns right, continue straight onto a two-lane, all-weather dirt road, and follow this road south along Adams Creek. Continue about 15 km (9 mi.) south on this road, just beyond the boundary of topographic map 72 F/12 Hungerford Lakes, and turn right (west) at the first opportunity. Turn right (north) again and back onto map 72 F/12 Hungerford Lakes on a two-lane, loose-surface road. Bear left and cross Adams Creek. Continue west another 3.5 km (2 mi.) and cross Battle Creek south of the site of the 1873 massacre. The road deteriorates after a small ranch house is passed, about 2.5 km (1.5 mi.) beyond Battle Creek.

The road from this point to the top of the Cypress Hills is keyed as "loose surface, dry weather," but the actual condition of the road is worse than one might imagine. The road has a poor base, and if it is wet, will be very soft. In this case, a four-wheel-drive vehicle is strongly recommended. The road continues through open range another 2.5 km (1.5 mi.) to the top of the hill, and another 4 km (2.5 mi.) to the highpoint. Again, a passenger vehicle may become stuck on this section if the road is wet. Total driving distance from Maple Creek is about 76 km (47.5 mi.).

The exact location of the highest point is not obvious, and probably will not be located without a careful survey. The point marked "4567" on map 72 F/12 Hungerford Lakes lies about 110 m (350 ft.) south of the road, but the land is very flat here, and a distance of 1.5 km (.9 mi.) may be travelled to the south before the 4550 foot contour line is crossed.

Contacts

Tourism Saskatchewan
500-1900 Albert Street, Regina, SK S4P 4L9
Phone: 1-800-667-7191

Additional Reading

"Prairie Oasis," Sid Marty, *Canadian Geographic,* Jan.-Feb. 1995, p. 46-59.

Unnamed Point

Prince Edward Island

149 m (457 ft.)
Lat/long N46° 20' 02" W63° 25' 16"
UTM 467600m.E. 5131000m.N. (NAD 27)
Topo map 11 L/6 & 11 L/11 North Rustico

Prince Edward Island is the smallest Canadian province and supports less than 0.1 per cent of the total population of Canada. PEI is sometimes called "The Garden of Canada," with extensive potato fields separating the picturesque towns and villages. The low, rolling landscape is covered with rich, red soil and red sandstone.

Prince Edward Island's highpoint, which has no name, is located about 25 km (15 mi.) northwest of Charlottetown. The 1:50,000-scale map North Rustico shows three separate areas above the 450 foot contour line. A recent survey has determined that the highest of these is the one adjacent to Highway 227 southeast of Glen Valley, and the 1991 publication of this map shows the highpoint as a benchmark about 100 m (330 ft.) from the road.

To reach the highpoint of Prince Edward Island, travel northwest from Charlottetown on Highway 2 about 26 km (16 mi.) to Fredericton. Turn south in Fredericton on Highway 264 and continue 3 km (2 mi.) to a junction with Highway 227 from Glen Valley. Turn left at the junction on the dirt road. Travel southeast onto a dirt road for approximately 900 m (2953 ft.) and park on the right at the boundary between a potato field and wood. Walk south along the boundary about 100 m (328 ft.) to the highpoint. The exact location of the highpoint is difficult to discern. It has been reported that a small rock cairn marks the exact point just inside the wood.

Contacts

Prince Edward Island Tourism
P.O. Box 940, Charlottetown, PEI C1A 7M5
Phone: 1-800-565-0267

Index